FRANCHISING FUNDAMENTALS

By: Fred Daphne

ACKNOWLEDGEMENTS

As **"Franchising Fundamentals: Your Guide to a Thriving Franchise Investment"** embarks on its journey into the world, I am overwhelmed with gratitude for the numerous individuals who have been integral to this endeavor.

At the forefront are you, the readers, whose pursuit of knowledge and dedication to growth are the very essence of this book's creation. I hope this guide proves invaluable in your path towards successful franchise ownership.

My team at Daphne Franchise Management Co. deserves immense recognition. Your unwavering commitment, insightful contributions, and relentless pursuit of excellence have not only shaped this book but also the core of our collective success.

A special acknowledgment goes to my mentors and business partners. Your guidance, wisdom, and steadfast support have been pivotal in my journey through the intricate landscape of franchising.

I am profoundly thankful to the exceptional team at Crimson Peak Publishing. Your expertise, meticulous attention, and dedication to crafting meaningful literature have been instrumental in bringing the spirit of "Franchising Fundamentals" to fruition. Collaborating with such a professional and personable team has been a privilege.

To my family and friends, whose unwavering love, patience, and encouragement have been my bedrock. You have continually inspired me to chase my passions with both heart and intellect.

"Franchising Fundamentals" is a testament to the collective effort, faith, and support of each one of you. My heartfelt appreciation for your invaluable contributions, and I am honored to share this accomplishment with you all.

Warm Regards,

Fred Daphne

CONTENTS

CHAPTER ONE
INTRODUCTION TO FRANCHISING

Franchising stands as a distinctive and accessible pathway to business ownership, merging the entrepreneurial zeal of an individual with the proven systems and brand power of an established business. This chapter introduces franchising as a dynamic business model, illuminating how it facilitates a symbiotic relationship between franchisors and franchisees. At its core, franchising involves licensing a business model and brand, allowing individuals to operate a business under an established brand name while benefiting from the support and systems provided by the franchisor.

The appeal of franchising spans a broad spectrum of investors, each drawn to its unique blend of autonomy and guided entrepreneurship. For seasoned business owners, franchising offers an opportunity to expand their portfolio and leverage their business acumen with reduced risk. The established business model, brand recognition, and franchisor support reduce the uncertainty and challenges typically associated with starting a business from the ground up. It presents a strategic avenue for diversifying investments and tapping into new markets or industries.

On the other end of the spectrum, franchising is equally appealing to new business owners, including those who may not have a robust background in business management. For these individuals, franchising serves as a gateway into the world of entrepreneurship, providing a structured framework and a safety net of support. This aspect is particularly attractive, as it lowers the barrier to entry for aspiring business owners who might feel overwhelmed by the prospect of starting a business independently. The training, operational systems, and ongoing support offered by franchisors play a crucial role in equipping these new entrepreneurs with the tools and confidence needed to manage and grow their business effectively.

As this chapter unfolds, we delve into the intricacies of the franchising model, exploring its various facets and how it caters to diverse investment profiles. From exploring the basics of franchising and its role in today's economy to aligning franchise opportunities with personal and professional goals, this chapter is designed to provide a comprehensive overview of franchising as a viable and attractive route to business ownership.

Understanding the Basics of Franchising

Franchising, as a business model, has a rich and varied history, tracing its origins back to the Middle Ages. However, it was not until the 19th century, with the rise of companies like Isaac Singer's sewing machine business, that franchising began to take the shape we recognize today. Singer's innovative approach to distributing his machines laid the foundation for modern franchising by allowing entrepreneurs to use his brand and business model in exchange for a fee. This system expanded rapidly in the 20th century, particularly in the United States, with the advent of the automobile and fast-food industries, marking the beginning of franchising as a major force in the global economy.

At its heart, franchising is a partnership between two key players: the franchisor and the franchisee. The franchisor owns the overarching brand and its associated trademarks, as well as the business system. They grant the franchisee the right to use these assets in return for a fee. This relationship is governed by a franchise agreement, a legal document outlining the terms of the partnership, including fees, territory rights, and the duration of the franchise.

The franchisor provides the franchisee with a proven business model, including training, support, and sometimes assistance with marketing and product supply. In turn, the franchisee operates the business independently but in accordance with the franchisor's guidelines. This relationship combines the franchisor's brand strength and system with the franchisee's local market knowledge and entrepreneurial spirit.

Franchises come in various forms, the most common being product distribution and business format franchising. Product distribution franchising, akin to a supplier-dealer relationship, involves the franchisee selling the franchisor's products. It is commonly seen in industries like automotive (e.g., car dealerships) and beverages.

Business format franchising, however, is more comprehensive. The franchisee not only sells the franchisor's products or services but also implements the franchisor's entire business format. This model is prevalent in numerous sectors, from fast food and retail to services like hotels and gyms.

Benefits and Challenges of Franchising

Benefits:

1. Proven Business Model: Franchising offers the franchisee a tried-and-tested business model, reducing the risk and uncertainty associated with starting a business from scratch.
2. Brand Recognition: Franchisees benefit from the established brand and customer base of the franchisor, which can take years to build independently.
3. Support and Training: Franchisors provide extensive training and ongoing support, helping franchisees navigate business operations effectively.
4. Economies of Scale: As part of a larger network, franchisees can enjoy cost benefits in procurement, marketing, and more.

Challenges:
* * *

1. Initial Investment: Franchising can require a significant upfront investment, though this varies widely across industries and specific franchises.
2. Ongoing Fees: Franchisees typically pay ongoing royalties and marketing fees, which can impact profit margins.
3. Less Autonomy: Franchisees must operate within the franchisor's system, which can limit creative freedom and business flexibility.
4. Market Saturation: In some areas, market saturation can limit growth potential, making location and franchise choice critical.

In conclusion, franchising offers a unique blend of independent ownership and supportive partnership. Its history of evolution has led to a diverse range of franchising opportunities, each with its unique benefits and challenges. For many entrepreneurs, the advantages of an established brand and support system make franchising an attractive alternative to starting a business from the ground up. However, it's crucial to weigh the initial investment and ongoing commitments against the potential rewards. Understanding these fundamentals can help prospective franchisees navigate the complexities of this dynamic business model.

The Role of Franchises in Today's Economy

The franchising model, a cornerstone of modern business, plays a pivotal role in shaping the global economy. Its influence extends far beyond individual entrepreneurs, impacting job creation, market dynamics, and economic development across diverse sectors. The economic footprint of franchising is immense and multifaceted, serving as a robust engine for growth and innovation.

Franchising's contribution to the global economy is staggering. In the United States alone, it is estimated that there are over 750,000 franchise establishments, generating over \$670 billion in economic output and employing millions of people. This represents approximately 3% of the U.S. GDP, a significant figure that underscores the impact of this business model. Globally, the influence of franchising extends into every corner of the market, from fast food and retail to healthcare and technology services. In countries like Australia, Canada, and across Europe, franchising is a key driver of economic activity, fostering entrepreneurship, and stimulating local economies.

The ripple effect of each franchise unit extends to various stakeholders - from suppliers and employees to customers and local communities. Franchises often serve as training grounds for budding entrepreneurs, equipping them with the skills to succeed in the broader business landscape. Moreover, franchising fosters diversity in entrepreneurship, opening doors for women, minorities, and veterans, who might otherwise face barriers in the business world.

The landscape of franchising is continually evolving, marked by emerging trends and growth patterns that reflect broader economic shifts. One significant trend is the increasing move towards technology integration. Many franchises are adopting digital solutions, from online ordering systems in food service to app-based customer interactions in retail and service industries. This digital shift is enhancing operational efficiency and customer engagement, proving crucial in an increasingly connected world.

Another notable trend is the rise of health and wellness franchises, spurred by growing consumer awareness and demand for healthier lifestyle choices. This sector has seen a surge in franchises offering fitness services, healthy eating options, and wellness products, highlighting a shift in consumer preferences and spending habits.

The global economy has also witnessed a growing interest in sustainable and eco-friendly franchises. More entrepreneurs are drawn to businesses that not only turn a profit but also positively impact the environment. This shift towards sustainability is opening up new opportunities in sectors like renewable energy, sustainable food, and green technologies.

Looking ahead, the franchising model is poised for continued growth, with sectors like technology, health, and sustainability leading the charge. The adaptability and resilience of the franchising model, even in the face of economic downturns, position it as a critical player in the global economy. As consumer preferences evolve and new technologies emerge, franchising is expected to adapt and grow, continuing its vital role in shaping economic landscapes worldwide.

In conclusion, the role of franchises in today's economy is significant and multifaceted. From contributing billions to the global GDP to setting trends in consumer markets, franchising remains a dynamic and influential business model. Its ability to adapt to changing economic conditions and consumer preferences ensures that it will continue to be a critical driver of growth and innovation in the global marketplace.

Aligning Franchise Opportunities with Personal and Professional Goals

The journey into franchising is more than a business decision; it's a personal endeavor that intertwines with an individual's aspirations and dreams. For many, franchising provides a pathway that aligns seamlessly with both personal goals and professional ambitions. This alignment is critical, as it's the harmony between these aspects that often dictates the success and fulfillment one finds in a franchise venture.

For those seeking a change from the 9-to-5 grind, franchising offers an enticing avenue for personal fulfillment. It presents an opportunity to be your own boss, have more control over your work-life balance, and pursue a passion. Franchisees often find that running their business aligns with their desire for autonomy, offering them the chance to make impactful decisions and reap the rewards of their hard work directly.

Moreover, franchising can fulfill the desire for a meaningful career. Many individuals choose franchises that resonate with their values and interests. For instance, someone passionate about health and wellness might find fulfillment in a fitness franchise. This alignment not only drives business success but also personal satisfaction, as franchisees see their work as an extension of their personal interests and values.

Professional growth is another crucial factor driving individuals towards franchising. Aspiring entrepreneurs often see franchising as a stepping stone to develop and showcase their leadership and management skills. A franchise provides a structured environment where one can grow a business with the support of a proven system. This is particularly appealing for individuals transitioning from corporate roles, looking to apply their skills in a new context.

Franchising also offers opportunities for continuous learning and development. Many franchisors provide comprehensive training programs and ongoing support, ensuring their franchisees are well-equipped to manage their businesses successfully. This aspect of franchising is attractive to individuals who value personal and professional growth and see it as a way to advance their careers.

Case Studies: Success Stories in Franchising

1. From Corporate Executive to Coffee Shop Owner

Mark, a former corporate executive in the tech industry, found his passion for coffee and community engagement unfulfilled in his 9-to-5 job. He turned to franchising and opened a coffee shop under a well-known brand. His background in management helped him excel in running the business, while his passion for coffee and community work brought personal satisfaction. Under his leadership, the coffee shop not only flourished financially but also became a beloved community hub.

2. Transforming Passion into Profit: The Fitness Franchisee

Sarah, a fitness enthusiast and former marketing professional, found her calling in a fitness franchise. Leveraging her marketing skills and passion for fitness, she created a fitness center that quickly stood out for its innovative programs and community-focused approach. Her story is a testament to how aligning personal passions with professional skills can lead to remarkable success in franchising.

3. Making a Difference: Education Franchise Success

* * *

John, a former teacher, always dreamt of having a bigger impact on education. He pursued his dream by investing in an education franchise. This allowed him to apply his educational expertise on a larger scale and fulfill his personal goal of shaping young minds. His franchise became known for its high-quality education and community impact, showcasing how personal goals can align seamlessly with professional aspirations in franchising.

Franchising stands out as a unique business model that caters to a diverse array of personal and professional goals. Whether it's seeking autonomy, pursuing a passion, or aspiring for professional growth, franchising offers a platform to turn these aspirations into reality. The success stories of franchisees across various industries underscore the potential of franchising to align with and fulfill both personal and professional objectives. For those contemplating a venture into franchising, understanding this alignment is key to not just achieving business success, but also personal satisfaction and professional fulfillment.

Self-Assessment for Potential Franchisees

Embarking on a franchise venture is akin to beginning a personal journey that demands not only financial investment but also a deep understanding of one's skills, strengths, and entrepreneurial spirit. For aspiring franchisees, self-assessment forms the bedrock of this journey, ensuring a match between one's abilities and the demands of franchising.

The first step in self-assessment involves a critical evaluation of personal skills and strengths. Prospective franchisees must ask themselves what skills they bring to the table. Are they adept at managing finances, marketing, or personnel management? Do they excel in customer service, or do they have a flair for strategic planning? Each franchise requires a unique set of skills, and understanding one's competencies can significantly impact the choice of franchise.

Interests play a crucial role too. Engaging in a franchise that aligns with personal interests can be more rewarding and sustainable in the long term. A passion for food might draw one towards a restaurant franchise, while a love for education could lead to investing in a tutoring business. This alignment not only ensures personal satisfaction but also drives motivation, especially during challenging times.

Assessing one's entrepreneurial mindset is another critical aspect of self-evaluation. Franchising requires a blend of independence and adherence to established systems. Potential franchisees must evaluate their comfort level with following a prescribed business model while also bringing in their entrepreneurial zeal to drive the business forward.

Readiness for the franchising journey goes beyond just willingness. It involves assessing one's ability to handle the pressures and responsibilities that come with running a franchise. This includes being prepared to make decisions, manage a team, and handle customer interactions effectively. One practical tool for assessing this readiness is the Entrepreneurial Aptitude Test (EAT), which evaluates traits such as risk tolerance, leadership ability, and adaptability.

Choosing the right franchise sector is pivotal. This decision should be based on a combination of personal interests, market trends, and financial considerations. For instance, a rapidly growing sector like health and wellness might be a lucrative option, but it requires a keen interest and understanding of the field.

Market research is vital in identifying suitable industries. Tools such as industry reports, market analysis, and franchise expos can provide insights into various sectors. Additionally, speaking with existing franchisees and industry experts can offer a real-world perspective on the demands and rewards of different franchises.

Case Studies: Aligning Skills and Interests with Franchise Choices

John's Journey to a Tech Franchise: John, a former IT professional, leveraged his technical skills and interest in technology to invest in a computer repair franchise. His background gave him a head start in understanding the business, while his passion for technology kept him engaged and motivated.

Maria's Leap into a Fitness Franchise: Maria, a fitness enthusiast with a background in sales, chose to invest in a fitness franchise. Her sales skills helped her in marketing her business effectively, while her love for fitness made her an authentic advocate for her franchise.

Alex's Adventure with an Art Franchise: Alex, who had always been passionate about art, decided to invest in an art studio franchise. His understanding of art and creativity added value to his business, attracting a niche clientele who appreciated his expertise.

Self-assessment is a fundamental step in the franchising journey. It requires potential franchisees to introspect and evaluate their skills, strengths, interests, and entrepreneurial readiness. Aligning these personal attributes with the right franchise sector can significantly enhance the chances of success and satisfaction in the franchising world. Aspiring franchisees should embrace this self-assessment process as a critical tool in their decision-making, ensuring that they embark on a franchising journey that is not only profitable but also fulfilling and aligned with their personal and professional aspirations.

Evaluating Financial Capabilities for Franchise Investment

Venturing into the world of franchising necessitates a keen understanding of one's financial capabilities. It's a balancing act between entrepreneurial dreams and fiscal realities. This chapter delves into evaluating one's financial status, understanding the investment requirements in franchising, exploring financing options, and drawing inspiration from real-life franchisee stories.

The initial step in assessing one's readiness for a franchise investment is a thorough evaluation of personal financial status. This involves analyzing current savings, income, debts, and other financial obligations. Prospective franchisees should prepare a detailed net worth statement, factoring in assets such as real estate, savings accounts, and retirement funds, against liabilities like loans and mortgages.

A crucial aspect is determining the amount of disposable income available for investment without jeopardizing personal financial stability. Financial advisors often recommend that potential investors should not invest more than 15-20% of their liquid assets in a franchise to mitigate risk. This cautious approach ensures that one's lifestyle and financial security are not compromised.

Franchising offers a spectrum of investment levels, from low-cost, home-based operations to high-investment, brick-and-mortar establishments. Initial investment costs typically include franchise fees, startup expenses, and working capital. These can range from a few thousand dollars for a small, service-based franchise to several hundred thousand dollars for a large retail franchise.

Understanding the total investment is vital. It's not just the initial franchise fee, but also the ongoing costs like royalties, marketing fees, and other operational expenses. Franchisors provide a detailed breakdown of these costs in their Franchise Disclosure Document (FDD), a crucial tool for potential franchisees to understand the financial requirements of the franchise.

Financing plays a pivotal role in making franchising accessible. Various financing options available include:

- Traditional Bank Loans: Banks offer loans specifically designed for franchise investments. However, securing a bank loan requires a solid business plan, good credit history, and sometimes collateral.

- SBA Loans: The Small Business Administration (SBA) provides loan programs with favorable terms, such as lower down payments and longer repayment periods. They are particularly beneficial for franchises listed in the SBA Franchise Directory.

- Franchisor Financing: Some franchisors offer in-house financing options to assist with the franchise fee or startup costs. These arrangements can be more streamlined, with potentially more favorable terms than traditional lenders.

- Alternative Financing: This includes home equity loans, retirement fund rollovers, and unsecured loans. While these can be viable options, they also carry risks and should be considered carefully.

Real-life Examples: Franchisees' Funding Journeys

Sarah's Home-Based Franchise Venture: Sarah, a former teacher, utilized her savings and a small bank loan to invest in a home-based education franchise. Her low overhead costs and the franchisor's support helped her break even within the first year.

Mike's Transition to a Fast-Food Franchise: Mike used a combination of personal savings and an SBA loan to purchase a fast-food franchise. His previous experience in the food industry and a strong business plan helped him secure the loan.

Linda's Creative Financing Approach: Linda, a corporate executive, tapped into her retirement funds through a Rollover for Business Startups (ROBS) scheme to invest in a fitness franchise. While this method was risky, it allowed her to avoid debt and retain more control over her business.

Raj's Partnership Model: Raj brought on two partners to share the financial burden of starting a high-investment retail franchise. This partnership not only eased individual financial strain but also brought diverse skills to the business.

In conclusion, evaluating financial capabilities for franchise investment requires an honest assessment of one's financial status, an understanding of the investment requirements, and exploring suitable financing options. Real-life stories of franchisees highlight that successful franchise investment is not reserved for the wealthy; with the right financial planning and strategies, it's within reach for many aspiring entrepreneurs. This journey, while challenging, opens doors to the world of business ownership, offering a unique blend of independence and support.

When embarking on the journey of franchising, thorough research stands as the cornerstone of success. For those navigating the franchising path, especially on a limited budget, understanding the market, franchisor background, legal intricacies, and financial aspects of franchising agreements is not just preliminary—it's essential.

Understanding the Market and Consumer Landscape

The first step in understanding the market is to dive deep into industry reports. These reports are treasure troves of data, offering insights into which franchising sectors are flourishing and which are facing challenges. They provide valuable information about market size, growth rates, and industry forecasts. For instance, an industry report might reveal a rising trend in health and wellness franchises or a surge in demand for home-based services. Such insights help you gauge which franchises are likely to thrive and align with future market demands.

Understanding what your potential competitors are doing is critical. This involves examining how they operate, their marketing strategies, customer service approaches, and product offerings. By analyzing your competitors, you can identify what works well and what doesn't, which can inform your strategy. For example, if you notice a competitor successfully implementing a unique loyalty program, it might inspire you to think about how you can incorporate similar strategies in your franchise. Similarly, understanding their shortcomings can help you fill gaps in the market.

While industry reports give you a macro perspective, understanding local market dynamics is about zooming in on the micro aspects. This involves getting a feel for the community where your franchise will operate. What are the local consumer behaviors? Are there cultural nuances that impact buying decisions? What is the economic environment like? For example, a franchise that thrives in an urban setting might not have the same success in a rural area. Understanding these nuances can guide you in choosing a franchise that resonates with the local community.

Market research in franchising goes beyond analyzing numbers and statistics; it's about understanding the psychology of your potential customers. What drives their purchasing decisions? What values do they hold dear? How do they perceive different brands? For instance, in today's market, there's a growing emphasis on sustainability and ethical practices. If these values align with the ethos of a franchise, it might attract a more loyal customer base. Understanding these underlying consumer sentiments can provide a competitive edge.

The culmination of effective market research is the ability to spot gaps in the market that your franchise can fill. This requires a combination of understanding consumer needs, analyzing competitor offerings, and being aware of emerging trends. Perhaps there's a growing demand for organic products in your area, but a lack of outlets offering them. Or maybe there's an opportunity for a service that leverages technology in a way that competitors haven't explored. Identifying these gaps is like finding uncharted territories in your ocean of opportunities, ripe for exploration and success.

In franchising, understanding the market and consumer landscape is about marrying data with intuition, blending statistical analysis with an understanding of human behavior. It's a dynamic process, requiring continuous learning and adaptation. As you embark on this endeavor, remember that your market research is not just a one-time task but an ongoing journey, evolving with the tides of the market. With each wave of information you ride, you get closer to selecting a franchise that not only survives but thrives in the vast ocean of

Delving into the Franchisor's World

Delving into the franchisor's world is an intricate process, akin to navigating through a labyrinth where each turn reveals crucial information about your potential business partner. Selecting the right franchisor involves piecing together various aspects of their business, much like assembling a complex puzzle. Each piece, whether it's their history, reputation, or financial stability, adds to the complete picture, helping you make an informed decision.

At the heart of this exploration is the Franchise Disclosure Document (FDD). Think of the FDD as a comprehensive blueprint that offers a transparent view into the franchisor's operations. It details everything from fees and obligations to the support provided by the franchisor. Delving into the FDD is like having a magnifying glass that lets you examine the fine print of your potential investment. It reveals the franchisor's litigation history, bankruptcy filings, and even earnings claims. Understanding the FDD is crucial; it's akin to reading the terms and conditions before signing a vital contract. It helps you gauge the franchisor's commitment to their franchisees and the level of support you can expect.

Another vital step is engaging in conversations with existing franchisees. These discussions can unveil the real-life experiences of running the franchise, far beyond what's outlined in any document. They are your window into the day-to-day operations, challenges, and successes of the business. Think of these conversations as customer reviews when you're purchasing a product. They provide honest insights into the franchisor's support, training effectiveness, and how policies play out in actual business scenarios. For instance, you might discover how responsive the franchisor is to queries or how effective their marketing strategies are in driving sales. This firsthand information is invaluable and can significantly influence your decision-making process.

Understanding the franchisor's financial stability is a critical part of this journey. It's like assessing the foundation of a house you're planning to buy. You need to ensure it's strong and won't crumble under pressure. This involves looking at their financial statements, understanding their revenue streams, and evaluating their growth and profitability. Are they financially sound enough to support expansion and invest in their franchisees? Do they have a sustainable business model? A financially robust franchisor is more likely to weather market fluctuations and provide continued support to its franchisees, which is crucial for your long-term success.

In summary, delving into the franchisor's world requires a

meticulous approach. It involves studying the FDD thoroughly, engaging with existing franchisees to understand the real-world application of franchisor policies, and evaluating the franchisor's financial health. Each of these steps is like a piece of a puzzle that, when put together, gives you a comprehensive view of what partnering with a particular franchisor entails. This process is crucial in ensuring that you choose a franchisor who not only matches your business goals but also has the capability and intention to support you in your entrepreneurial

Navigating the Legal and Financial Maze

Navigating the legal and financial aspects of a franchising agreement is a complex yet critical journey, akin to finding your way through a multifaceted maze. Each turn in this maze represents a new legal obligation or financial commitment that demands your attention and understanding. From deciphering the intricacies of territorial rights and renewal terms to balancing the financial costs against potential returns, every step in this process shapes the future of your franchise venture.

Legal obligations within the franchise agreement are diverse, encompassing territorial rights, renewal terms, and more. These terms define the operational boundaries and longevity of your franchise. For instance, territorial rights set the exclusive area for your operations, while renewal terms dictate the conditions for extending your business relationship with the franchisor. Understanding these legalities is crucial, as overlooking them can lead to future complications and missteps.

On the financial front, the agreement presents a labyrinth of commitments, including initial fees, ongoing royalties, and marketing costs. These financial obligations must be carefully weighed against the expected returns of the franchise. A thorough analysis of the franchisor's financial history, revenue models, and profit projections is essential to ensure that your investment yields satisfactory returns and that the costs do not overshadow the benefits.

* * *

Consulting with professionals specialized in franchise law and financial planning is indispensable. A franchise lawyer acts as your guide, helping navigate the legal terms, identify potential red flags, and protect your interests. Similarly, a financial advisor assists in evaluating the viability of financial commitments and developing a robust financial strategy. Their expert guidance is akin to a map through the maze, ensuring that your foray into franchising is both legally sound and financially viable. With their support, you can confidently embark on your franchising journey, equipped to unlock its potential and steer towards success.

Leveraging Resources for Informed Decision-Making

The journey of researching and selecting the right franchise is a multifaceted adventure, one that requires thorough exploration and informed decision-making. This process is significantly enriched when you leverage a variety of resources available to potential franchisees. Each of these resources plays a unique role in providing insights and guidance, helping you make a choice that aligns with your aspirations and capabilities.

Franchise expos and events serve as vital platforms where you can immerse yourself in the world of franchising. These events offer more than just information; they provide an opportunity for direct interaction with franchisors. You can engage in conversations, ask pressing questions, and gain a tangible feel of different franchise models. These events often feature a range of franchisors, from established brands to emerging opportunities, allowing you to compare and contrast various options in one setting.

In today's digital age, online forums and social media groups have become indispensable tools. These platforms are akin to a modern-day agora – bustling marketplaces of ideas and experiences where current and prospective franchisees exchange insights, advice, and support. Participating in these online communities can offer you real-time feedback, diverse perspectives, and a sense of camaraderie with others embarking on similar entrepreneurial journeys.

* * *

Industry reports and trade publications offer a broader perspective of the franchising landscape. They provide valuable data on market trends, growth sectors, consumer behaviors, and economic forecasts. This bird's-eye view is crucial for understanding the macroeconomic factors that could impact your franchise choice. By staying informed about the latest developments and projections in the franchising world, you can make strategic decisions that are not only grounded in current realities but also poised to capitalize on future opportunities.

Lastly, franchise consultants offer personalized guidance tailored to your specific situation and goals. These professionals can help you navigate the complexities of the franchising process, from identifying suitable opportunities to analyzing franchise agreements. Their expertise can be particularly beneficial in aligning your personal aspirations, financial capabilities, and market opportunities. A consultant's role can be likened to that of a trusted advisor, providing customized advice and helping you avoid common pitfalls.

In summary, leveraging these diverse resources is crucial for making an informed franchise decision. Whether it's the interactive learning at expos, the community wisdom of online platforms, the strategic insights from industry reports, or the personalized guidance from consultants, each resource contributes to a comprehensive understanding of franchising. By effectively utilizing these tools, you can embark on your franchising journey with confidence, equipped with the knowledge and insights needed for success.

Research in franchising is a narrative of exploration, discovery, and understanding. It's about piecing together different elements of the franchising puzzle to form a clear picture. This comprehensive approach helps prospective franchisees make informed decisions, laying a strong foundation for a successful and fulfilling franchising journey. As you turn the pages of this guide, remember that each step in your research is a step toward realizing your entrepreneurial dreams in the world of franchising.

Preparing for the Franchising Journey

Embarking on a franchising journey is akin to setting sail on a vast entrepreneurial sea. To navigate these waters successfully, meticulous preparation is key. This preparation involves developing a robust business plan, building a strong support system, and setting realistic expectations about the challenges and rewards of franchising.

Developing a Comprehensive Business Plan

The first step in your preparation is crafting a comprehensive business plan. This document is your roadmap, outlining your path from inception to success. A well-structured business plan for a franchise should include several key components:

Executive Summary: This section provides an overview of your business plan, summarizing key points like your mission statement, business model, and core objectives.

Market Analysis: Dive deep into market research, understanding your target audience, industry trends, and competitor analysis. This insight is crucial in positioning your franchise effectively in the market.

Operational Plan: Detail the day-to-day operations of your franchise, including staffing, suppliers, and daily management practices. This plan should align with the franchisor's guidelines while being tailored to your specific location and market.

Marketing Strategy: Develop a comprehensive marketing strategy that encompasses both franchisor-provided marketing tools and your own initiatives. This strategy should cover how you intend to attract and retain customers.

Financial Projections: A critical part of your business plan is financial forecasting. Include projections for revenue, expenses, cash flow, and break-even analysis. These projections should be realistic and based on thorough market research.

No franchise owner is an island, and building a network of support is vital. Networking with other franchisees and industry experts can provide invaluable insights and guidance. Attend franchising events, join online forums, and participate in local business groups to connect with others in the franchising community.

* * *

Seek mentorship from experienced franchisees who can offer practical advice and share their experiences. They can provide tips on everything from negotiating with suppliers to effective local marketing strategies. Additionally, consider building relationships with industry experts such as franchise consultants, financial advisors, and legal experts who can offer specialized guidance.

Finally, it's essential to set realistic expectations for your franchising journey. Franchising offers a structured pathway to business ownership, but it also comes with its set of challenges. Be prepared for a significant time investment, especially in the initial stages of setting up your franchise. Understand that success may not be immediate, and the first few months or even years can be a learning curve.

Mentally and practically prepare for the demands of franchising. This includes being ready to adapt to franchisor guidelines, managing staff, and dealing with day-to-day operational challenges. Embrace continuous learning and be open to adapting your strategies based on market feedback.

In summary, preparing for your franchising journey requires a combination of strategic planning, network building, and mindset preparation. A comprehensive business plan lays the groundwork, a strong support system provides the backbone, and realistic expectations set the stage for a rewarding franchising experience. With these elements in place, you are well-equipped to embark on a successful franchising voyage

Conclusion

As we draw this chapter to a close, it's vital to reflect on the key points we've traversed in our introduction to the world of franchising. The journey we've embarked on is not just about business; it's about aligning entrepreneurial dreams with practical strategies, setting the stage for a successful and fulfilling franchising venture.

* * *

Recap of Key Points

We began by unraveling the basics of franchising, understanding it as a unique blend of entrepreneurial independence and structured support. We dived into the history and types of franchising, appreciating how this model has evolved and diversified over time. The significance of franchising in today's economy was highlighted, demonstrating its impactful role in global commerce and as a catalyst for individual wealth creation.

Aligning personal and professional goals with franchising opportunities emerged as a crucial theme. We saw how franchising could be a conduit for achieving personal aspirations and professional growth, as illustrated through inspiring case studies. The chapter stressed the importance of self-assessment for prospective franchisees, encouraging an introspective approach to gauge entrepreneurial readiness and industry preferences.

Evaluating financial capabilities was another focal point, guiding readers through assessing their financial status and exploring various financing avenues. The chapter also emphasized the indispensable role of research in making informed franchising decisions, from conducting market analysis to understanding legal and financial aspects of franchise agreements.

Finally, we discussed the necessity of preparing for the franchising journey. This preparation involves developing a comprehensive business plan, building a network of support, and setting realistic expectations for the road ahead.

To those standing at the threshold of this exciting venture, remember that franchising is a journey of continuous learning and adaptation. Embrace the challenges as opportunities for growth and be steadfast in your commitment to your goals. Leverage the support and resources available to you, and don't hesitate to seek guidance when needed. Franchising, with its blend of structure and autonomy, offers a unique platform to build your success story.

As we move forward, the upcoming chapters will delve deeper into the practicalities and strategies of successful franchising. We'll explore how to meticulously select a franchise that aligns with your goals, the intricacies of negotiating and finalizing franchise agreements, and the keys to managing and growing your franchise business effectively. We will provide insights into marketing strategies, staff management, and customer service excellence, all crucial components of running a successful franchise.

CHAPTER TWO

FINDING THE RIGHT

FRANCHISE OPPORTUNITY

In the intricate tapestry of franchising, the act of choosing the right franchise is the cornerstone of potential success or failure. Chapter 2 of our journey into the realm of franchising pivots around this crucial choice, delving deep into the art and science of selecting a franchise that resonates with an investor's personal and financial aspirations.

Embarking on a franchise venture is like navigating a vast sea of opportunities, each with its unique challenges and rewards. The importance of this choice cannot be overstated. A well-chosen franchise can be a conduit to financial success, personal fulfillment, and professional growth. Conversely, a mismatched franchise can lead to unmet expectations and financial strain. Therefore, it's imperative to approach this decision with a meticulous, informed, and strategic mindset.

This chapter is crafted to serve as your compass in this pivotal decision-making process. We will begin by exploring the diverse landscape of franchise industries – from the bustling world of food and beverage to the innovative realms of technology and services. Each industry comes with its distinct trends, growth trajectories, and inherent risks. Understanding these nuances is vital in aligning your choice with market dynamics and personal interests.

However, the journey doesn't stop at industry selection. We delve deeper, guiding you through evaluating franchise opportunities that align with your budget. Budgetary constraints should not be a barrier to entering the world of franchising. We aim to demonstrate how various franchises cater to a spectrum of financial capabilities, offering opportunities for both modest and substantial investments.

Determining a franchise's profit potential is another critical aspect we will explore. This involves dissecting financial statements, understanding earnings projections, and evaluating market positioning. We will draw upon real-life case studies to illustrate how profitability is influenced by a myriad of factors – from the choice of location to the strength of the brand and the saturation of the market.

Moreover, for those cautious about significant initial investments, we will highlight franchises known for their low entry barriers. Whether it's home-based opportunities or mobile services, these low-investment franchises present an accessible pathway into business ownership. Yet, they also come with their set of considerations which we will examine in detail.

Finally, the chapter concludes with an action plan, a step-by-step guide to kickstart your franchise selection process. This plan will include practical tools, checklists, and strategies for evaluating and comparing different franchise options, preparing you for the exciting yet daunting task of choosing the franchise that best suits your aspirations.

In summary, Chapter 2 is about equipping you with the knowledge and tools to make a choice that sets the foundation for a successful and rewarding franchising journey. Let's embark on this crucial phase of your franchising adventure, where informed decisions lead to flourishing businesses.

Finding Your Franchise

As we delve deeper into the world of franchising, assessing the vast array of industries available for investment becomes a pivotal task. Each industry, from the bustling food sector to the dynamic world of services, offers unique opportunities, growth trajectories, and inherent challenges. This section of our journey is dedicated to navigating these diverse waters, helping you align your choice with both personal passion and market viability.

The franchising universe is as varied as it is vast. At one end lies the food and beverage industry, a sector synonymous with franchising itself. Renowned for brands that range from fast-food giants to niche coffee shops and specialty foods, this industry is often the first that comes to mind when one thinks of franchising. However, its popularity also means high competition and market saturation in certain areas.

Then there's the retail sector, encompassing everything from clothing stores to specialized equipment suppliers. Retail franchising offers the allure of tangible products and direct customer interaction but often requires a significant upfront investment in inventory and storefronts.

Service-based franchises, including sectors like home services, education, and healthcare, present a different kind of opportunity. These industries often require less physical infrastructure than retail, potentially lowering initial investment costs. Moreover, the growing demand for personal and professional services provides a fertile ground for growth.

Emerging industries shouldn't be overlooked. The rise of technology and the shift towards sustainability have spawned innovative franchise opportunities in IT services, renewable energy, and eco-friendly products. These emerging sectors offer the excitement of being at the forefront of market trends and consumer shifts.

Industry-Specific Trends, Growth, and Risks

Understanding the specific trends and growth patterns within these industries is crucial. The food industry, for instance, is seeing a shift towards health-conscious dining and fast-casual experiences. Retail is being transformed by e-commerce, demanding a hybrid approach to physical and online presence. Service industries are increasingly leveraging technology to enhance efficiency and customer experience.

However, with these trends come specific risks. The food industry faces challenges like fluctuating food costs and changing health regulations. Retail must constantly innovate to stay relevant in an e-commerce-dominated era. Service industries require continuous improvement of skills and staying updated with technological advancements.

Choosing an industry should be a reflection of your personal interests and market demand. Are you passionate about food and hospitality? Then the food and beverage industry might be your calling. Do you have a knack for retail, a sense of style, and a pulse on consumer trends? Retail franchising could be your arena. Or perhaps your interests lie in providing services that make a difference in people's lives – here, sectors like education or home services offer rewarding opportunities.

Market demand is equally important. A deep understanding of local market needs and consumer behavior is essential. For instance, a community with a high number of families might be ripe for educational and childcare services. An area with an aging population could offer opportunities in healthcare and home services.

Assessing different franchise industries requires a blend of self-reflection and market analysis. It's about finding where your passions intersect with market opportunities. As you explore these industries, consider not just the current trends and risks but also the long-term viability and how they align with your personal and professional goals. Remember, the right choice is one that not only promises financial returns but also resonates with your values and interests, setting you on a path to both professional success and personal fulfillment in the franchising world.

Strategies for Finding Franchises at Different Budget Levels

Evaluating franchise opportunities within your budget is a task that requires a strategic blend of financial acumen and diligent research. It's about identifying franchises that not only align with your financial capabilities but also promise a viable return on investment. This part of your franchising journey involves navigating through various budget levels, understanding the nuances of franchise cost breakdowns, and mastering the art of cost-benefit analysis.

Franchises come in a wide range of investment levels, from low-cost, home-based options to high-end, brick-and-mortar establishments. Here are some strategies to find the right fit:

Define Your Budget: Start by determining your investment range. Consider your available liquid capital, how much you're willing to finance, and your comfort level with the investment amount.

Research Extensively: Utilize franchise directories and online resources that categorize franchises by investment level. Attend franchise expos and webinars, where you can gather information about various opportunities within your budget.

Consider Emerging Brands: While established franchises might require higher investment, newer or less known brands often have lower entry costs. These emerging franchises can offer untapped market potential but may carry higher risks.

Explore Diverse Industries: Don't limit yourself to popular or familiar industries. Sometimes, less obvious choices might offer more affordable opportunities that align well with your budget and market demand.

Understanding Cost Breakdowns of Typical Franchises

The cost of a franchise involves several components beyond the initial franchise fee. Here's a breakdown:

- Initial Franchise Fee: This one-time fee grants you the license to use the franchisor's brand and system. It can range from a few thousand to several hundred thousand dollars, depending on the brand.

- Operational Costs: These include expenses for setting up your business, like real estate (purchase or lease), equipment, initial inventory, and staffing. Operational costs vary greatly depending on the franchise model and location.

- Ongoing Fees: Franchisees typically pay ongoing royalties (a percentage of revenue or a fixed fee) and contribute to a national marketing fund. These fees cover the ongoing support, training, and brand promotion provided by the franchisor.

- Additional Costs: Consider costs such as insurance, local marketing, maintenance, and technology upgrades.

Conducting a Cost-Benefit Analysis

A cost-benefit analysis is crucial in evaluating whether a franchise investment makes financial sense. Here's how to approach it:

Estimate Total Investment: Calculate the total cost of starting and operating the franchise for the first year, including the franchise fee, setup costs, and working capital.

Analyze Revenue Projections: Use the Franchise Disclosure Document (FDD) and discussions with existing franchisees to estimate potential revenues. Be cautious and consider best, average, and worst-case scenarios.

Consider Long-Term Financial Implications: Assess the long-term profitability of the franchise. How long will it take to break even? What are the projected earnings after the initial few years?

Compare with Alternatives: Weigh the potential return of the franchise investment against other investment options. Is investing in a franchise the best use of your capital considering the risk and return?

Seek Professional Advice: Consult with a financial advisor or an accountant experienced in franchising. They can provide valuable insights into the financial feasibility of your potential investment.

Evaluating franchise opportunities within your budget is a multifaceted process. It involves not just understanding the financial requirements but also carefully analyzing the potential return on your investment. By employing strategic research, understanding the comprehensive cost breakdown, and conducting a thorough cost-benefit analysis, you can identify a franchise opportunity that fits your budget and offers promising financial prospects. Remember, the goal is to find a balance between financial commitment and potential rewards, paving the way for a successful and sustainable franchise venture.

Determining The Franchise's Profit Potential

Determining a franchise's profit potential is a critical step in the franchising journey. It involves examining various factors that influence the success and profitability of a franchise operation. Understanding these elements helps in making an informed decision about whether a particular franchise can meet your financial goals and aspirations.

Location: The adage "location, location, location" holds true in franchising. The profitability of a franchise can be heavily dependent on its geographical setting. Factors like foot traffic, visibility, accessibility, and the demographics of the area play a significant role. For instance, a fast-food franchise located in a busy urban area with high foot traffic is likely to see different profit margins than one in a quieter suburban location.

Brand Strength: The strength and recognition of the franchise brand are crucial. A well-established brand with a loyal customer base can significantly contribute to a franchise's success. Brand strength affects customer trust and can lead to higher sales volumes. However, it's important to balance this with the cost of investing in a high-profile franchise, which can be substantially higher.

Market Saturation: Understanding the level of market saturation is vital. Entering a market with an oversupply of similar franchises or services can lead to fierce competition and lower profits. On the other hand, identifying a franchise in a niche market or a location with unmet demand can offer more lucrative opportunities.

Operating Costs: Evaluating the operating costs, such as staffing, supplies, utilities, and rent, is essential. Lower operating costs can lead to higher profit margins, but they must not come at the expense of quality and customer satisfaction.

Understanding Financial Statements and Earnings Claims

Financial Statements: Reviewing the franchisor's financial statements, specifically the Franchise Disclosure Document (FDD), gives insight into the financial health of the franchise system. Pay attention to items like the initial investment, ongoing fees, average sales figures, and any disclosed financial performance of existing units.

Earnings Claims: Some franchisors provide earnings claims or financial performance representations in their FDD. These can offer a glimpse into the potential revenues and profits of the franchise. However, it's important to approach these claims critically, understanding they are averages or estimates and may not reflect your individual experience.

Due Diligence: Conducting due diligence by talking to existing franchisees can provide real-world insights into the profitability of the franchise. They can share their experiences regarding revenues, expenses, and profitability, which can be more telling than theoretical figures.

Case Studies of Successful Franchises

* * *

Chick-Fil-A: As the fast food franchise with the highest profit margins,. an analysis of its profitability revealed that factors like a prime location in a bustling city center, strong brand recognition, and efficient operations contributed to its high profit margins. Despite high initial investment and operational costs, the franchise benefitted from consistent customer traffic and a strong marketing strategy by the franchisor.

Ideal Siding: A retail franchise specializing in eco-friendly products demonstrated success through strategic location choices in environmentally conscious communities and leveraging the growing trend of sustainability. The brand's unique market position and strong community engagement led to higher-than-average sales figures and profitability.

Home Clean Heroes: A home cleaning service franchise capitalized on an underserved market in suburban areas. By maintaining low operational costs and providing exceptional service, this franchise achieved profitability within the first year of operation, outperforming initial projections.

In conclusion, determining a franchise's profit potential is a multi-faceted process that requires careful consideration of location, brand strength, market saturation, operating costs, and an in-depth analysis of financial statements and earnings claims. By examining these factors critically and learning from the success stories of other franchises, prospective franchisees can gauge the potential profitability of a franchise and make a decision that aligns with their financial objectives. Remember, while historical data and case studies are valuable, your success will also depend on your management skills, market conditions, and the level of support from the franchisor.

Identifying Franchises with Low Initial Investment Requirements

When it comes to stepping into the franchising world, particularly for those with limited resources, identifying franchises with low initial investment requirements can be a gateway to entrepreneurship. These types of franchises offer unique opportunities, balancing affordability with potential for success.

Home-based franchises are a prime example of low-investment options. Operating from the owner's home, these franchises eliminate the need for a physical commercial space, significantly reducing startup and operational costs. They encompass a wide range of services, from consulting and virtual tutoring to online marketing. The appeal lies in their simplicity and the ability to start quickly with minimal overhead. Check out this link for an overview of some home-based franchises (https://www.franchisedirect.com/home-based-franchises/?gad_source=1&gclid=CjwKCAiA75itBhA6EiwAkho9e9ttqv0RuMo8WAoPBI0r2waq80WzCfwxrZQyLfva7qEc7oNQ8_zAfRoCUF8QAvD_BwE)

Another attractive option is mobile services. These businesses are characterized by their "go-to-the-customer" model, requiring no fixed storefront. Mobile service franchises can include anything from pet grooming services that visit clients' homes to mobile car repair services or cleaning services. The beauty of this model lies in its direct engagement with the customer in their own space, offering convenience and personalized service. Here is an overview of some mobile service franchises like All Dry Services, Window Gang, DoodyCalls, and more (https://www.franchisedirect.com/sitesearch/?search_term=mobile%20services)

Online businesses also present lucrative opportunities for low-investment franchising. E-commerce franchises, for instance, leverage the vast reach of the internet to sell products or services. Similarly, digital marketing agencies operate primarily online, minimizing the need for physical inventory or large office spaces.

While the low initial investment aspect of these franchises is enticing, it's important to consider the pros and cons. On the positive side, these franchises typically involve reduced financial risk, making them ideal for individuals cautious about investing large sums. They also offer flexibility in terms of working hours and locations, which can be appealing for those seeking a work-life balance. The operational demands are usually simpler, too, often requiring fewer employees and less inventory management.

However, there are challenges. Some low-investment franchises may have limited growth potential, especially when compared to larger franchises that require more capital. The ease of entry in these sectors can lead to high competition, making it imperative for franchisees to differentiate themselves effectively. Additionally, running a home-based or mobile franchise requires a high degree of self-motivation and discipline, as the traditional structures and routines of an office or store setting are absent.

For those looking to maximize returns with minimal initial investment, a few strategies are key. Conducting thorough market research to identify unmet needs and market gaps is crucial. Selecting a franchise that not only fits the current market demand but also has potential for future growth can set the stage for long-term success. Leveraging technology is another crucial aspect, especially for online and mobile franchises. Digital tools for marketing, customer relationship management, and operational efficiency can significantly enhance reach and streamline processes.

In essence, low-investment franchises offer a unique blend of affordability, flexibility, and entrepreneurial opportunity. They are especially suited for individuals looking to dip their toes into the franchising world without the burden of heavy initial investments. With careful planning, research, and the right use of technology, these franchises can grow into profitable and rewarding businesses.

Action Plan for Beginning Your Franchise Journey

Embarking on a franchise journey is an exhilarating venture, blending the thrill of entrepreneurship with the structure of a proven business model. For those ready to take this path, having a well-defined action plan is crucial. This guide aims to provide a step-by-step framework, complete with checklists and tools, to assist you in starting the franchise selection process and preparing for those all-important initial discussions with franchisors.

* * *

Step 1: Define Your Goals and Criteria

Before diving into the ocean of franchising opportunities, it's essential to anchor yourself with a clear understanding of what you seek to achieve. Ask yourself:

- What are my long-term professional goals?
- What level of involvement do I desire in my business?
- What are my financial limitations and investment capacity?
- Which industries align with my interests and skills?

Answering these questions will help you create a personal criterion that will be instrumental in filtering through various franchise options.

Step 2: Industry Analysis

The next step involves a deep dive into different industries. Utilize tools like industry reports, market analysis, and online resources to understand the trends, growth potential, and risks associated with various sectors. Consider not only current market data but also future projections and potential market shifts.

Step 3: Research Franchise Options

Armed with industry insights, begin exploring specific franchise opportunities. Use a variety of resources:

- Franchise directories offer comprehensive listings.
- Franchise expos and seminars provide opportunities to meet franchisors and gather firsthand information.
- Online forums and discussion groups can offer candid insights from current franchisees.

Step 4: Initial Franchise Evaluation

As you gather a list of potential franchises, start a preliminary evaluation based on your defined criteria. Create a checklist for each franchise that covers:

- Initial investment requirements

- Franchise fees and ongoing royalties
- Brand reputation and track record
- Support and training offered
- Market presence and competition

Step 5: Deep Dive into Selected Franchises

Narrow down your list to a few top choices and delve deeper:

- Request and review the Franchise Disclosure Document (FDD) for detailed information on the franchisor, the franchise system, and legal obligations.
- Conduct site visits to existing franchise locations.
- Speak with current franchisees to get unfiltered feedback on their experience.

Step 6: Financial Viability Assessment

Evaluate the financial aspects of your shortlisted franchises. This step may involve:

- Analyzing cost breakdowns and potential revenue streams.
- Conducting a cost-benefit analysis to weigh the investment against potential returns.
- Consulting with financial advisors to understand the implications of your investment.

Step 7: Preparing for Franchisor Meetings

As you prepare to meet with franchisors, equip yourself with a set of questions and discussion points. This should include queries about:

- Training and support structures
- Marketing and advertising assistance
- Territory rights and exclusivity
- Performance benchmarks and success stories
- Exit strategies and resale policies

Step 8: Legal Consultation

* * *

Before making any commitments, consult with a franchise attorney. They can help you:

- Understand the legal terms of the franchise agreement
- Identify any potential red flags in the FDD
- Negotiate terms, if possible

Step 9: Final Decision Making

With all the information and advice at hand, take the time to reflect and decide. Ensure that your choice aligns with your goals, financial capacity, and lifestyle preferences.

Step 10: Steps Post Decision-Making

Once you've made your decision, the journey is just beginning. The next steps involve:

- Finalizing the franchise agreement
- Securing financing, if required
- Planning for business setup – location, hiring, training, etc.

Tools and Checklists

To streamline your process, consider using or developing the following tools:

Franchise Comparison Spreadsheet: Create a spreadsheet to compare your shortlisted franchises side by side based on various criteria.

Franchise Evaluation Checklist: Develop a checklist for evaluating each franchise, which can be filled out during your research. Develop a weighted scale based on your personal priorities

Questions for Franchisor Template: Prepare a template of questions to ask franchisors during meetings.

* * *

Financial Assessment Tool: Use or develop a tool for financial analysis of your potential franchise investment.

Beginning your franchise journey is a process filled with excitement, learning, and crucial decision-making. By following a structured action plan, utilizing various tools and checklists, and seeking professional advice, you can navigate this path with greater confidence and clarity. Remember, the key to a successful franchise venture lies not only in choosing the right franchise but also in thorough preparation and informed decision-making. With patience, diligence, and the right resources, you can set the stage for a rewarding and prosperous franchising career.

As we conclude Chapter 2 of our franchising journey, it's time to reflect on the rich tapestry of insights and strategies we've woven together. This chapter has been a compass, guiding you through the intricate process of selecting the right franchise, a decision that blends personal aspirations with practical realities.

The Journey So Far...

We began this chapter by assessing the diverse world of franchise industries. From the bustling energy of food services to the innovation-driven tech sector, each industry presents unique opportunities and challenges. We delved into industry-specific trends, discussing how aligning your personal interests with market demand can lead to a fulfilling and profitable franchise venture.

Understanding the financial aspect of franchising was our next milestone. We explored strategies to find franchises fitting different budget levels, dissecting the cost breakdowns of typical franchises. This financial awareness is vital; it's the foundation upon which your franchise dream is built.

Then, we journeyed into determining the profit potential of franchises. We analyzed factors influencing a franchise's profitability, from the strategic significance of location to the strength of the brand and market saturation. Case studies of successful franchises illuminated these concepts, offering real-world examples of profitability metrics.

Identifying franchises with low initial investment requirements was another critical focus. We highlighted franchises known for lower initial investments, like home-based businesses and mobile services. The balance between minimal initial investment and maximizing returns was a recurring theme, showcasing how a lean start can lead to lucrative outcomes.

As you stand at this juncture, equipped with knowledge and strategies, it's time to stride forward confidently into the next phase of your franchising journey. Remember, the process of selecting the right franchise is both an art and a science. It requires an alignment of your passions, strengths, and financial capabilities with the right franchising opportunity.

Let this chapter serve as your guide and your inspiration. The journey of selecting a franchise is personal and unique. It's a reflection of who you are, your dreams, and how you envision your future in the world of business.

As we venture into Chapter 3, we delve deeper into the franchise selection and evaluation process. This next chapter is where your dreams start taking a more concrete shape. We'll explore the nuances of evaluating franchise opportunities, examining the franchisor-franchisee relationship, and understanding the legal and operational aspects of franchising agreements.

In Chapter 3, we focus on:

- **Detailed Evaluation of Franchise Opportunities:** Learn how to scrutinize franchise opportunities with a fine-tooth comb. We'll discuss how to evaluate the franchisor's business model, support systems, and training programs.

- **Understanding the Franchisor-Franchisee Relationship:** Gain insights into what makes a successful franchisor-franchisee partnership. We'll talk about the expectations, commitments, and the synergies required for a successful collaboration.

- **Navigating Franchise Agreements:** Get equipped with the knowledge to navigate the complexities of franchise agreements. Learn about the legalities, your rights as a franchisee, and the critical clauses to watch out for.

As you close this chapter and prepare to open the next, reflect on your franchising aspirations. Take the time to absorb the insights shared, and start laying the groundwork for the crucial decisions ahead. Research, reflect, and be ready to ask the tough questions.

Your franchising journey is about more than just starting a business; it's about realizing a dream and sculpting a future that aligns with your vision. As you move into the heart of the franchise selection process in Chapter 3, do so with confidence, armed with the knowledge and insights you've gained. Franchising is a journey of discovery, growth, and, ultimately, fulfillment. The path you choose now will shape your entrepreneurial story. Embrace this journey with an open mind and a committed heart, and let the adventure begin.

CHAPTER THREE

FINANCING OPTIONS FOR FRANCHISEES WITH LIMITED CAPITAL

Chapter 3 of our guide, "Financing Options for Franchisees with Limited Capital," embarks on a crucial aspect of the franchising journey: securing the financial means to realize entrepreneurial dreams. This chapter opens up with an in-depth look at the pivotal role that financing plays in the world of franchising, especially for individuals who have the drive and vision but are constrained by limited capital.

The realm of franchising presents a unique blend of opportunities and challenges, and one of the most significant hurdles faced by many aspirants is the aspect of financing. The introduction of this chapter underscores the importance of understanding and navigating the various financing options available to franchisees. It brings to light the fact that while franchising offers a structured pathway to business ownership, the initial investment and ongoing financial commitments can be daunting, particularly for those who do not have substantial savings or easy access to traditional funding sources.

For prospective franchisees operating with a tighter budget, this chapter serves as a beacon of hope and guidance. It acknowledges the challenges these individuals face - from meeting the initial franchise fees to managing the operational costs once the business is up and running. The introduction sets the stage for a deep dive into the diverse financial landscapes of franchising, highlighting the importance of each option in empowering franchisees to overcome financial barriers.

This section of the book does more than just list out financing options; it aims to equip readers with the knowledge to make informed decisions about which financial paths are best suited to their personal circumstances and business goals. It is a crucial segment for those who dream of owning a franchise but feel hindered by their financial limitations. The chapter promises to unravel the complexities of financing, offering insights into traditional and innovative funding avenues, and provides a detailed exploration of how to approach and secure these funding sources.

In essence, this introduction paves the way for an enlightening journey through the world of franchise financing. It is designed to inspire confidence and provide practical solutions, ensuring that the dream of owning a franchise remains accessible and achievable, even for those with limited capital.

Exploring Traditional Financing Options: Bank Loans and SBA Loans

In the landscape of franchising, securing adequate funding is often the linchpin to transforming entrepreneurial aspirations into tangible business ventures. Traditional financing options, particularly bank loans and Small Business Administration (SBA) loans, stand out as pivotal avenues for aspiring franchisees, especially those with limited capital.

Old Faithful: Bank Loans

Bank loans, as a conventional financing option, play a significant role in enabling franchise ownership, especially for first-time franchisees. Their straightforward nature, coupled with the assurance of structured repayment plans, makes them a viable choice for many. However, navigating the path to securing a bank loan requires a nuanced understanding of the lending process, eligibility criteria, and the impact of various factors on loan terms.

When it comes to franchising, banks typically look for certain key elements in a loan application. The borrower's creditworthiness is paramount, as it indicates the likelihood of loan repayment. A strong credit score, often above 700, significantly enhances the chances of loan approval and can lead to more favorable interest rates.

Banks also scrutinize the business plan presented by the franchisee. A well-thought-out business plan that showcases market research, clear financial projections, and a solid understanding of the franchise model is crucial. It should detail the operational strategy, marketing plans, and provide a realistic financial forecast for the franchise.

Another important aspect is collateral. Banks often require collateral as a security measure for the loan, which could include assets like real estate, investment accounts, or other valuable properties.

The interest rates on bank loans for franchises can vary based on the lender, the borrower's credit history, and the economic climate. As of late 2023, typical interest rates for small business loans ranged from 3% to 7%. However, rates can fluctuate, and it's advisable for potential franchisees to shop around and negotiate with various lenders to secure the best rate.

Repayment terms for franchise loans usually span five to ten years, but this can vary based on the loan amount and the specific agreement with the lender. Longer repayment terms can lower monthly payments but might increase the total interest paid over the life of the loan.

Success Story: Leveraging Bank Loans for Franchise Success

John's journey in securing a bank loan for his fast-food franchise exemplifies the effectiveness of this financing route. With a strong credit score and a compelling business plan, John managed to secure a loan at a competitive rate. His success story highlights the importance of thorough preparation and understanding the nuances of bank loans.

John's approach included:

- Developing a comprehensive business plan that demonstrated his understanding of the fast-food industry and outlined his strategies for success.
- Maintaining a strong credit score, which he achieved by managing his previous debts responsibly and ensuring a good credit history.
- Choosing the right bank that had a history of funding franchises and offered terms that matched his financial capacity.

Tips for Prospective Franchisees Seeking Bank Loans

1. Start by reviewing your credit report and score, addressing any discrepancies and working to improve your score if necessary.
2. Research and select a bank that has experience in franchising and offers competitive rates.
3. Prepare a detailed, well-researched business plan that includes market analysis, projected financials, and a clear operational strategy.
4. Consider possible collateral and understand the implications of using personal assets as security for the loan.
5. Consult with a financial advisor or a loan officer specializing in franchise financing to navigate the process effectively.

In summary, securing a bank loan for a franchise requires a strategic approach, encompassing a strong personal financial foundation, a convincing business plan, and the selection of a suitable lender. By understanding and navigating these elements

SBA Loans: A Tailored Solution for Small Businesses

* * *

In the journey of franchising, securing the necessary capital can often be the most challenging step, particularly for individuals with limited resources. The Small Business Administration (SBA) offers a beacon of hope for such entrepreneurs through its specialized loan programs. These loans, designed to cater specifically to the needs of small businesses and franchises, provide more accessible and advantageous options than traditional bank loans.

The SBA loans are characterized by lower down payments, extended repayment terms, and more flexible eligibility criteria. Unlike conventional bank loans, SBA loans are not directly funded by the agency but are guaranteed through participating lenders. This guarantee significantly reduces the risk for lenders, thereby easing the path for small business owners to obtain financing. For franchisees, these loans can be a game-changer, offering the financial backing needed to kickstart their business ventures.

To qualify for an SBA loan, franchisees must meet specific criteria set by the agency. This includes operating for profit within the United States, having a reasonable amount of invested equity, and demonstrating a need for the loan. The application process is rigorous and requires a well-crafted business plan, financial projections, and proof of the ability to repay the loan. Franchisees must navigate this process with precision, ensuring that every document and detail aligns with the SBA's requirements.

A shining example of the effectiveness of SBA loans in the franchising world is seen in the story of Sarah, who aspired to open a children's education franchise. Facing the challenge of limited personal capital, Sarah turned to an SBA 7(a) loan for assistance. The loan, which can provide funds ranging from a few thousand dollars to $5 million, was perfect for covering most of her initial franchise costs. Despite the intricate nature of the loan application process, Sarah's determination and thorough preparation paid off, resulting in a successful funding that laid the foundation for her business.

Sarah's success story is not an isolated case. Many franchisees have leveraged SBA loans to overcome financial barriers, proving that these loans can be a vital tool in realizing entrepreneurial ambitions. The

SBA loans, particularly the 7(a) and 504 programs, have facilitated countless small businesses in their growth and expansion. These loans are not just financial aids; they are catalysts for turning dreams into tangible businesses.

In conclusion, both bank loans and SBA loans offer viable pathways for financing a franchise. While bank loans provide a more traditional route, SBA loans offer a tailored solution with potentially more favorable terms for small businesses. Success stories like those of John and Sarah serve as testaments to the efficacy of these traditional financing options. For aspiring franchisees, understanding and navigating these options can be the first step towards realizing their entrepreneurial dreams. The key lies in thorough preparation, understanding the nuances of each option, and aligning them with one's financial capabilities and business objectives.

Utilizing Government Programs and Grants

When it comes to financing a franchise, government programs and grants can be a lifesaver for those with limited capital. These offerings provide an alternative to traditional loans, often featuring more favorable terms for small business owners. This section delves into federal and state programs, grants, and how prospective franchisees can tap into these resources.

Federal and state governments recognize the importance of small businesses in driving economic growth and offer various programs to support their development. The U.S. Small Business Administration (SBA) is a pivotal agency in this realm, offering a plethora of programs tailored to small businesses, including franchises. These programs range from loan guarantees to training and market development assistance.

The SBA's loan programs are particularly noteworthy for franchisees. With lower down payments, longer repayment terms, and flexible eligibility criteria, these loans can be more attainable than traditional bank financing. The SBA doesn't directly lend money; instead, it guarantees loans made by participating lenders, reducing

45

the risk and making it easier for small businesses to get financing.

Grants for Franchising

While less common than loans, grants offer an attractive funding option as they don't need to be repaid. Federal and state agencies, along with private companies, provide small-business grants. For instance, Grants.gov is a comprehensive database of federal small-business grants across various agencies. These grants support a range of enterprises, from environmental conservation to childcare services.

The SBA's Small Business Innovation Research (SBIR) and Small Business Technology Transfer (STTR) programs are excellent examples of grant opportunities that focus on research and development in technology and scientific research. These programs connect entrepreneurs with federal grants and contracts from 12 government agencies.

Securing a grant can be a competitive process, but the rewards are worth the effort. Potential franchisees should start by identifying grants for which they qualify. This could be based on the industry, location, or the owner's background. Grants.gov and SBA's website are invaluable resources for researching available grants.

The application process for these grants can be intricate, requiring detailed proposals and compliance with specific requirements. For instance, the USDA's Rural Business Development Grant, which supports small businesses in rural areas, requires applicants to be located in eligible rural areas and meet certain employee and revenue criteria.

Government programs and grants offer viable alternatives to traditional financing, particularly for franchisees with limited resources. By leveraging these opportunities, prospective franchisees can overcome financial barriers, bringing them closer to realizing their entrepreneurial

* * *

Innovations in Financing: Crowdfunding and Peer-to-Peer Lending

In the ever-evolving landscape of franchise financing, crowdfunding and peer-to-peer lending have emerged as innovative solutions, particularly beneficial for those with limited capital. These modern financing methods break down traditional barriers and open up new avenues for funding.

Crowdfunding has revolutionized the approach to franchise financing. It allows individuals to raise small amounts of capital from a large number of people, typically via the internet. This method not only provides the necessary funds but also fosters a community of supporters who are invested in the success of the business.

Popular crowdfunding platforms like Kickstarter, Indiegogo, and Fundable have transformed the way entrepreneurs fund their ventures. Kickstarter, known for its project-based funding approach, has seen over 155,000 projects funded with over $4.1 billion pledged. Indiegogo offers a diverse range of funding options, including campaign extensions and equity crowdfunding, catering to a wide array of business needs.

Franchises have successfully leveraged crowdfunding to raise capital. For example, a franchise like System4, a commercial cleaning service, could be initiated for as little as $6,200, making it an ideal candidate for crowdfunding. Other low-cost franchises like Cruise Planners-American Express Travel, requiring under $3,000 to start, or Jazzercise, Inc., which can be initiated for around $4,000, also present feasible options for crowdfunding.

The key to a successful crowdfunding campaign lies in effective storytelling and community engagement. Franchisees need to articulate their vision, how the franchise will benefit the community, and the value it will bring to investors. Promotions through social media and local networking play a critical role in driving the campaign's success.

* * *

Peer-to-Peer Lending: Personalized Financing Options

Peer-to-peer (P2P) lending is another innovative financing method. It connects potential franchisees directly with individual lenders, bypassing traditional financial institutions. This model offers more personalized loan agreements, often with competitive interest rates.

Platforms like LendingClub and Prosper have paved the way for P2P lending, providing an alternative for those who may not qualify for conventional loans. These platforms facilitate loans for various purposes, including business financing, and often provide more flexible terms than traditional banks.

The advantages of P2P lending include potentially lower interest rates and a more streamlined application process. However, it's crucial for borrowers to be aware of the risks involved, such as the possibility of higher interest rates for those with lower credit scores and the lack of a physical institution to negotiate with in case of financial difficulties.

Crowdfunding and peer-to-peer lending represent the forefront of financing innovation for franchisees. These methods provide viable alternatives to traditional funding sources, especially for those with limited capital. They not only offer financial solutions but also engage communities and individual investors in the success of the franchise. As the franchising landscape continues to evolve, these financing options stand as testament to the adaptability and resilience of the entrepreneurial spirit. Prospective franchisees should explore these avenues, considering their unique benefits and challenges, to find the best fit for their financial needs and business goals.

Negotiating with Franchisors for Flexible Payment Terms

In the quest to open a franchise, negotiating with franchisors for flexible payment terms can be a game-changer, especially for entrepreneurs with limited capital. This section dives into effective strategies for negotiating payment terms, showcases real-life examples of successful negotiations, and explores the various types of flexible payment options available.

The art of negotiation with franchisors begins with thorough preparation and a clear understanding of your financial limitations. It's essential to approach these discussions with a well-thought-out plan, highlighting your strengths as a potential franchisee and the mutual benefits of flexible payment terms.

Before entering negotiations, research the franchisor's history of offering flexible payment terms. Understand their usual terms and conditions and prepare to propose an arrangement that aligns with your financial capabilities. Make a compelling case by showcasing your relevant experience, business acumen, and market knowledge. Highlight how your skills and dedication can contribute to the franchise's success. Recognize that franchisors are also looking for a beneficial deal. Be prepared to discuss how flexible payment terms can lead to a long-term profitable partnership for both parties. Articulate your proposal clearly, outlining how the flexible terms will enable you to maximize the franchise's potential without overstretching your finances. Approach the conversation with flexibility, being open to counteroffers and adjustments.

Real-Life Examples of Successful Negotiations

The Fast-Food Franchisee: John, a prospective franchisee of a fast-food chain, successfully negotiated a reduced initial franchise fee and a phased payment plan. By presenting a strong business plan and demonstrating his market understanding, John convinced the franchisor of his potential for long-term success, leading to a mutually beneficial agreement.

The Retail Franchise Negotiation: Sarah, interested in a retail franchise, negotiated a lower royalty fee for the first year. She underscored her retail management experience and proposed a higher royalty rate after the initial period, once the business had established itself.

* * *

Franchisors, recognizing the challenges faced by franchisees with limited capital, often offer various flexible payment options. These can range from deferred payment plans to reduced initial fees. Some franchisors allow franchisees to start their business and defer the initial franchise fee payment to a later date. This option can be especially beneficial for businesses that need time to generate revenue. In certain cases, franchisors may offer a reduced initial fee, lowering the entry barrier for new franchisees. This reduction can free up capital for other startup expenses. Franchisors might offer reduced royalty fees during the initial phase of the business, allowing franchisees to reinvest more profits back into the business for growth. Additionally, some franchisors link payment terms to the franchise's performance, creating an incentive-based structure that aligns with the franchisee's success.

Case Studies: Benefits

Emily's Coffee House Franchise

Background: Emily, an entrepreneur with limited capital, wanted to open a franchise of a popular coffee house chain. Concerned about the substantial initial investment, she approached the franchisor to discuss flexible payment options.

Negotiation Strategy: Emily prepared a detailed business plan showcasing her market research, financial projections, and a strategic plan for local marketing. She emphasized her strong management background and her commitment to the brand.

Outcome: The franchisor was impressed with Emily's preparation and her clear vision for the franchise. They agreed to a reduced initial franchise fee and allowed her to pay the remaining fee in installments over two years. This arrangement enabled Emily to manage her finances effectively while establishing her franchise.

Raj's Fast-Food Franchise

Background: Raj was interested in opening a fast-food franchise but was hesitant due to the high upfront costs and royalty fees.

Negotiation Strategy: Raj proposed a performance-based royalty fee plan, where he would pay a lower royalty rate initially, which would gradually increase as the franchise's sales grew. He supported his proposal with a thorough analysis of the local market and sales projections.

Outcome: The franchisor, recognizing the potential in Raj's proposal and his analytical approach, agreed to the performance-based royalty plan. This flexible arrangement allowed Raj to focus on growing his business without the pressure of high fees in the early stages.

Linda's Fitness Center Franchise

Background: Linda, a fitness enthusiast, wanted to bring a new fitness center franchise to her community. However, the high costs of equipment and initial setup were barriers.

Negotiation Strategy: Linda requested the franchisor to assist in financing the gym equipment. She highlighted her extensive network in the local fitness community and her marketing plan to quickly establish the brand in her area.

Outcome: The franchisor agreed to lease the equipment to Linda for the first year, reducing her initial capital requirement. This creative solution helped Linda launch her fitness center with manageable financial commitments.

Kevin's Educational Franchise

Background: Kevin, a former teacher, sought to open an educational franchise. With limited resources, he needed a flexible financial arrangement to start his business.

Negotiation Strategy: Kevin presented a staggered payment plan, where he would pay a small portion of the franchise fee upfront and the rest from the business's revenue over the first three years.

Outcome: Impressed by Kevin's passion for education and his

comprehensive business plan, the franchisor agreed to the staggered payment plan. This arrangement allowed Kevin to leverage his expertise in education while managing his financial constraints effectively.

Each of these case studies exemplifies how prospective franchisees can successfully negotiate flexible payment terms with franchisors. By presenting well-thought-out proposals and highlighting their strengths and commitment, these entrepreneurs were able to secure terms that aligned with their financial capabilities and business goals.

Creative Financing Solutions

Creative financing solutions offer a lifeline for aspiring franchisees, especially those with limited capital. Navigating through the financial constraints to realize the dream of owning a franchise can be challenging, yet achievable with innovative approaches. Two such solutions are forming partnerships and leveraging personal assets. Each comes with its unique set of considerations, risks, and strategies.

Entering into a partnership is a strategic way to pool resources and share the financial burden of starting a franchise. Partnerships can bring together individuals with complementary skills and financial strengths, multiplying the potential for success. However, they require careful planning and clear agreement.

The foundation of a successful partnership in franchising lies in a well-structured partnership agreement. This document should outline each partner's financial contribution, roles, responsibilities, and profit-sharing ratios. It's essential to clearly define how decisions will be made, how profits and losses will be distributed, and under what conditions a partner can exit the business. Legal advice is crucial in drafting this agreement to ensure all partners are protected and the terms are enforceable.

Case Study: Tech Franchise Partnership

John and Mike, both with IT backgrounds but limited capital, decided to partner and open a tech franchise. They structured their partnership agreement to reflect John's higher financial contribution, granting him a larger share of the profits but also a larger share of the risk. Mike contributed his extensive technical expertise. This balanced approach led to a successful partnership, with the franchise growing steadily in profitability and market presence.

Using personal assets to finance a franchise is another viable option for many entrepreneurs. This approach includes tapping into savings, retirement funds, home equity, or other personal investments. While it can be a quick way to raise capital, it also carries significant risks.

Risks and Benefits:

The primary benefit of using personal assets is the immediate availability of funds without the need to seek external financing. It offers more control over the business since there are no external lenders or partners involved. However, the risks include potential loss of personal savings, impact on retirement funds, and the possibility of losing personal property if the business fails.

To minimize these risks, prospective franchisees should:

Assess the Franchise's Viability: Conduct thorough research into the franchise's success rate, market demand, and competitive landscape. A well-chosen franchise with a proven track record can reduce the risk of failure.

Diversify Funding Sources: Instead of relying solely on personal assets, consider combining them with other financing options. This diversification can reduce personal risk.

Set Aside Emergency Funds: Ensure that not all personal savings are invested into the franchise. Maintaining an emergency fund can provide a safety net.

* * *

Get Expert Advice: Consult financial advisors to understand the implications of using personal assets for business purposes. They can provide insights into risk management and optimal use of personal finances.

Case Study: Home-Based Franchise Success

An example of successfully leveraging personal assets is Laura's story. Laura, a marketing professional, decided to invest her savings into a home-based marketing franchise. She conducted extensive market research and chose a franchise with low overhead costs and a strong brand presence. To mitigate risks, she used only a portion of her savings, keeping the rest as a safety net. Her strategic approach paid off, as her franchise quickly gained traction, allowing her to recoup her investment within two years.

Structuring Personal Asset Utilization

When using personal assets, it's crucial to structure their utilization strategically. For instance, if leveraging home equity, one should calculate the monthly payments and ensure they align with the projected cash flow of the franchise. Similarly, when using retirement funds, one should understand the tax implications and the impact on future retirement plans.

Franchisees should also consider the long-term effects of using personal assets. It's essential to have a plan for replenishing these assets over time. This could involve setting aside a portion of the franchise's profits to rebuild personal savings or making additional contributions to retirement funds.

Case Study: Leveraging Retirement Funds

Take the case of David, who used a portion of his retirement funds to open a fast-food franchise. Aware of the risks, he worked with a financial planner to understand the tax implications and develop a plan to replenish his retirement savings from the franchise's profits. His calculated risk was rewarded when his franchise became profitable, allowing him to not only replenish his retirement funds but also expand his franchise portfolio.

Creative financing solutions like partnerships and leveraging personal assets offer powerful means to launch a franchise, especially for those with limited external funding options. The key to success in these approaches lies in careful planning, risk assessment, and strategic decision-making. By balancing the benefits and risks and leveraging expert advice, prospective franchisees can utilize these creative financing solutions to turn their entrepreneurial dreams into reality. As they embark on this journey, it's crucial to remain vigilant about the financial implications and to always have a contingency plan in place. With the right strategy, creative financing can pave the way for a successful and sustainable franchise venture.

Conclusion

As we conclude this chapter on financing options for franchisees with limited capital, it's important to reflect on the diverse avenues explored and the opportunities they present for aspiring entrepreneurs. From traditional bank and SBA loans to innovative methods like crowdfunding and peer-to-peer lending, each option offers unique advantages and challenges. We also delved into the realm of negotiating flexible payment terms with franchisors and employing creative solutions like partnerships and leveraging personal assets.

For those embarking on this franchising journey, the key takeaway is the importance of being open to a variety of financing strategies. The landscape of franchise financing is rich and varied, and finding the right fit requires a willingness to explore and understand each option. This exploration is not just about securing the necessary funds; it's about crafting a financial strategy that aligns with your goals, risk tolerance, and long-term vision for your franchise.

* * *

As we turn the page to the next chapter, we shift our focus to selecting and evaluating a franchise. This next phase of your journey is about aligning your entrepreneurial ambitions with the right franchise opportunity. We'll cover how to assess a franchise's market potential, understand its operational model, and evaluate its fit with your personal and professional goals. The upcoming chapter will provide you with the tools and insights to make an informed decision, one that sets the foundation for your success as a franchisee.

Additional Resources

To further assist you in your franchising journey, here is a list of resources that can provide additional guidance and support:

Financial Advisors and Consultants Specializing in Franchising:

FranFund: Specializes in franchise funding solutions (www.franfund.com)
BoeFly: Offers assistance with franchise financing and loan matchmaking (www.boefly.com)
The Franchise Consulting Company: Provides financial advice and franchise consultation (www.thefranchiseconsultingcompany.com)

Websites and Platforms for Crowdfunding and Peer-to-Peer Lending:

- Kickstarter: A popular platform for crowdfunding various projects, including business ventures (www.kickstarter.com)
- Indiegogo: Offers a flexible crowdfunding platform suitable for a wide range of businesses (www.indiegogo.com)
- LendingClub: A leading peer-to-peer lending platform that connects borrowers with investors (www.lendingclub.com)

Links to Government Programs and Grant Opportunities for Small Businesses:

- **U.S. Small Business Administration:** Offers various loan

programs and resources for small businesses (www.sba.gov)
- **Grants.gov**: A comprehensive database of federally funded grants, including those for small businesses (www.grants.gov)
- **SCORE:** Provides free business mentoring and education, with a focus on helping small businesses get off the ground (www.score.org)

These resources are invaluable tools in your franchising journey, offering guidance, financial assistance, and the insights necessary to navigate the complexities of franchise financing. As you explore these options and move forward in your journey, remember that the path to successful franchising is paved with informed decisions, strategic planning, and a steadfast commitment to your entrepreneurial vision. The world of franchising is vast and full of potential, and with the right approach, your dream of owning a successful franchise is well within reach.

CHAPTER FOUR

LEGAL AND CONTRACTUAL ASPECTS OF FRANCHISING

Franchising, a dynamic avenue for business expansion and entrepreneurship, necessitates a keen understanding of its legal and contractual landscape. This chapter introduces the multifaceted legal dimensions that underpin franchising, setting the stage for a comprehensive exploration of franchise agreements, legal terminologies, and regulatory compliance. Here, we delve into why these elements are not just formalities but critical pillars that uphold the franchising structure.

At its core, franchising is a legal relationship between a franchisor, who owns the overarching business model and brand, and a franchisee, who purchases the right to operate a business under these pre-established parameters. This relationship, governed by intricate contracts and legal stipulations, forms the bedrock of a successful franchise operation. Understanding these legalities is crucial for both parties to ensure their business ventures are not just profitable but also legally sound and compliant.

The franchise agreement, a cornerstone document in this journey, encapsulates the terms of the relationship. It's a detailed contract that lays out rights and obligations, fees, territory delineations, duration, renewal conditions, and much more. Given its complexity and long-term implications, grasping the nuances of these agreements is vital. They dictate how a franchise operates, the financial commitments involved, and the extent of control exerted by the franchisor.

Furthermore, these agreements encompass provisions for protecting the brand identity, a critical aspect for franchisors to maintain uniformity and reputation across different locations.

Another critical aspect covered in this chapter is the legal terminology inherent in franchising. Terms like 'franchise fees', 'royalties', 'exclusivity', and 'territorial rights' are not merely contractual jargon but pivotal components that define the scope and profitability of a franchise. Understanding these terms is essential for prospective franchisees to evaluate the feasibility and potential of a franchise opportunity accurately.

Compliance with regulatory standards plays a significant role in franchising. In the United States, for instance, the Federal Trade Commission (FTC) requires franchisors to provide a Franchise Disclosure Document (FDD) to prospective franchisees. This document, packed with information about the franchisor, the franchise system, and the legal and financial aspects of the franchise, is a critical tool for due diligence. It ensures transparency and equips franchisees with the information needed to make informed decisions.

Moreover, franchising laws vary considerably from state to state, adding another layer of complexity. These variations necessitate an understanding of both federal and state-specific legal frameworks. This is where the role of specialized legal advisors becomes indispensable. They guide both franchisors and franchisees through the intricacies of these agreements, ensuring compliance and safeguarding against potential legal pitfalls.

In essence, the legal and contractual aspects of franchising are much more than mere formalities. They are the pillars that support the entire franchising structure. By dissecting these elements, this chapter aims to provide a comprehensive guide for those embarking on the franchising journey. It highlights the importance of meticulous scrutiny, informed decision-making, and the need for expert legal counsel in navigating the complex but rewarding world of franchising. Through this deep dive, potential franchisees and franchisors can gain the clarity and confidence needed to foster successful, compliant, and mutually beneficial franchise relationships.

* * *

Understanding Franchise Agreements

In the realm of franchising, the franchise agreement stands as the cornerstone document, defining the relationship between the franchisor and the franchisee. This legally binding contract delineates the rights, responsibilities, and roles of both parties, forming the basis for a structured and regulated business partnership.

A franchise agreement is a legal contract that establishes the terms under which a franchisor grants the rights to a franchisee to operate a business under the franchisor's brand and system. The essence of this agreement lies in its dual purpose: firstly, to protect the franchisor's intellectual property and business model, and secondly, to provide a clear framework within which the franchisee can operate, grow, and succeed.

The franchisor-franchisee relationship, governed by this agreement, is unique in business. Unlike a typical employer-employee relationship, it offers the franchisee a level of autonomy in running the business, yet within the confines of the franchisor's established systems and guidelines. This balance is crucial as it allows for the consistency and quality control necessary for the brand's reputation, while also giving the franchisee the opportunity to grow a business with an established brand and support system.

The franchise agreement encompasses various clauses and sections, each playing a pivotal role in shaping the franchising experience. Some of the key components include:

Franchise Fees and Royalties: This is one of the most crucial elements of the agreement. The franchise fee is a one-time payment made by the franchisee to the franchisor, usually at the outset, granting access to the franchisor's brand and system. Royalties, on the other hand, are ongoing payments, typically calculated as a percentage of the franchisee's sales, paid for ongoing support, training, and the use of the franchisor's trademark and business system. Understanding these fees is fundamental for the franchisee to assess the financial viability of the venture.

* * *

Territory Rights and Exclusivity: Territory rights define the geographical area in which the franchisee is allowed to operate. This section of the agreement is critical as it can impact market saturation and competition among franchises. Some agreements may grant exclusive rights to a territory, while others might allow the franchisor to open additional franchises within the same area. The specific terms can greatly affect a franchisee's potential customer base and revenue.

Duration and Renewal Terms: The length of the franchise agreement, typically ranging from 5 to 20 years, dictates how long the franchisee can operate under the franchisor's brand before the contract needs renewal. This section also outlines the conditions and terms under which the agreement can be renewed, which is vital for long-term business planning for the franchisee.

Operational Standards and Brand Guidelines: To maintain brand consistency, franchisors set strict operational guidelines that franchisees must follow. These include store layout, design, product or service quality standards, pricing, marketing strategies, and even employee uniforms. Adherence to these standards is essential to uphold the franchisor's brand integrity and customer experience across different locations.

Training and Support: Franchisors often provide initial training and ongoing support to franchisees. This section of the agreement specifies the extent, duration, and nature of the support, which can include marketing, operational guidance, staff training, and technology support. This clause is critical for franchisees, especially those new to the industry, as it outlines the level of assistance they can expect from the franchisor.

Advertising and Marketing: This component details the franchisee's obligations regarding marketing and advertising. It may include mandatory participation in national or regional advertising campaigns, contributions to an advertising fund, and guidelines for local marketing efforts. Understanding these requirements is important for franchisees as they impact both the budget and the promotional strategies of the franchise.

Supply Chain and Approved Suppliers: Franchisors often mandate that franchisees purchase supplies, inventory, or equipment exclusively from approved suppliers. This ensures uniformity in product quality across all franchise locations. This section of the agreement will detail these requirements and how they must be fulfilled.

Renewal, Termination, and Transfer Clauses: These clauses outline the conditions under which a franchise agreement can be renewed, terminated, or transferred. Understanding these terms is crucial for both parties, as they determine the future of the franchise relationship. This includes conditions under which a franchisee can sell or transfer the franchise and the franchisor's right to terminate the agreement.

Dispute Resolution and Governing Law: In case of disagreements or legal disputes, the franchise agreement should specify the mechanisms for resolution. This often includes arbitration or mediation procedures and identifies the governing law which will apply to the agreement.

Financial Performance Representations: Some franchise agreements may include financial performance representations, giving prospective franchisees an idea of potential sales, profits, or earnings. However, franchisors are not required to provide these details, and when they do, they must have a reasonable basis for their claims and provide written substantiation.

Insurance and Liability: This section outlines the insurance requirements for the franchisee, which may include liability, property, and workers' compensation insurance. The franchisor may also clarify the extent of liability coverage that the franchisee must maintain.

In conclusion, a franchise agreement is a detailed and comprehensive document that requires careful scrutiny. Prospective franchisees must understand each component and its implications on their business operations. It's often advisable to seek the expertise of a legal professional experienced in franchising to navigate the complexities of these agreements. By thoroughly understanding the franchise agreement, franchisees can enter into the franchising relationship with a clear perspective of their rights, responsibilities, and the path to success within the franchising framework.

Key Terms and Clauses in Franchise Contracts

Franchise contracts are complex documents filled with critical terms and clauses that define the franchisor-franchisee relationship. These terms cover a wide range of aspects from financial commitments to operational guidelines. Understanding these key terms is essential for anyone considering entering into a franchise agreement.

Franchise fees and royalties represent the financial backbone of the franchising model. The franchise fee is an upfront cost paid by the franchisee to the franchisor. This fee, which can range significantly based on the franchise, typically covers the right to use the franchisor's name and system, initial training, support in setting up the franchise, and access to the franchisor's proprietary knowledge and materials.

Royalties, on the other hand, are ongoing payments made by the franchisee to the franchisor. Usually calculated as a percentage of the franchisee's gross sales, royalties are meant to compensate the franchisor for ongoing support and the continued use of the brand and system. Royalties can also be a fixed amount, independent of sales, but this is less common. These payments often fund services such as national advertising campaigns, technology upgrades, and new product development, which benefit the entire franchise system.

Territory Rights and Exclusivity

Territory rights and exclusivity are critical in determining where and how a franchisee can operate. Territory rights define the geographic area within which a franchisee can operate and market their business. These can be exclusive, meaning the franchisor agrees not to establish any other franchises or operate competing units in the designated area, or non-exclusive, which may allow the franchisor to open additional units in the same territory.

Exclusivity clauses are particularly crucial as they protect franchisees from internal competition within the franchise system. However, the specifics of territorial rights can vary widely between franchises, and understanding these nuances is essential for franchisees, especially when operating in densely populated or highly competitive markets.

Operational Standards and Brand Guidelines

Operational standards and brand guidelines are the heart of a franchise's consistency and success. These clauses ensure that every franchise unit, regardless of location, maintains the same look, feel, and quality as the original. Operational standards can include specifics on store layout, product or service offerings, pricing, employee uniforms, and customer service protocols.

Brand guidelines go beyond mere aesthetics; they encompass the overall brand identity, including trademarks, logos, and marketing materials. Adherence to these standards is critical to maintain brand integrity and customer expectations across all locations. Violations can not only damage the brand but also result in legal repercussions for the franchisee.

Renewal, Termination, and Transfer Clauses

Understanding the terms related to the renewal, termination, and transfer of the franchise agreement is crucial for long-term business planning and stability.

Renewal Clauses: These provisions outline the conditions under which a franchise agreement can be renewed at the end of its term. They may include performance criteria, renovation or modernization requirements, and additional fees. It's important for franchisees to understand these terms well in advance of the expiration of the agreement to prepare for any stipulations or financial obligations required for renewal.

Termination Clauses: Termination clauses specify the conditions under which either party can end the franchise agreement prematurely. Common grounds for termination by the franchisor include non-compliance with operational standards, failure to pay royalties, or breach of contract. For franchisees, there may be provisions for termination if the franchisor fails to provide support or uphold their end of the agreement. Understanding these conditions is essential for both parties to protect their investments and mitigate risks.

Transfer Clauses: These clauses govern the franchisee's ability to sell or transfer their franchise to a third party. Transfer clauses typically require franchisor approval for any sale or transfer and may include conditions such as the franchisor's right of first refusal, transfer fees, or requirements for the new owner to complete franchisor training programs. These terms ensure that any new franchisee is capable and willing to uphold the franchise's standards and operations.

The key terms and clauses in franchise contracts form the foundation of the franchisor-franchisee relationship. They define the financial commitments, operational guidelines, and the boundaries within which the franchisee must operate. Understanding these terms is not just about legal compliance; it's about grasping the essence of what it means to be part of a franchise system.

Franchise fees and royalties determine the economic model of the franchise. Territory rights and exclusivity clauses protect the franchisee's market while maintaining the franchisor's network integrity. Operational standards and brand guidelines ensure uniformity and quality across all locations, which is vital for customer trust and brand reputation. Renewal, termination, and transfer clauses outline the life cycle of the franchise agreement, providing clarity on how the relationship can evolve and adapt over time.

For prospective franchisees, comprehending these terms is crucial for making an informed decision about entering into a franchise agreement. It's advisable to seek legal and financial advice to fully understand the implications of these clauses. For franchisors, clearly defined and well-communicated terms are essential for maintaining a strong, compliant, and successful franchise network. Ultimately, a well-structured franchise agreement benefits both parties, leading to a prosperous and enduring business relationship.

The Role of Legal Advisors in Franchising

Franchising, as a complex business model, intertwines legal, financial, and operational elements, necessitating expert guidance. Legal advisors play a pivotal role in this arena, offering specialized knowledge that is crucial for both franchisors and franchisees. Understanding their importance, how to select the right attorney, and the specific ways they can assist is vital for anyone entering the franchising world.

The intricacies of franchise agreements and the regulatory environment surrounding franchising make legal counsel not just an option, but a necessity. Franchise agreements are legally binding documents, often dense with industry-specific terms and conditions. Misinterpretation or oversight can lead to costly legal disputes or business failures.

Legal advisors provide expertise in interpreting and navigating the complex legal landscape of franchising. They ensure compliance with federal and state laws, such as the Federal Trade Commission's (FTC) rules and the Franchise Disclosure Document (FDD) requirements. Their understanding of the legal nuances helps protect parties from unintended liabilities and ensures that the franchise agreement is fair, transparent, and aligned with both parties' interests.

Selecting a Franchise Attorney

When it comes to selecting a franchise attorney, the decision is crucial for both prospective franchisees and franchisors. The first step in this process is to ensure that the attorney specializes in franchise law. This area of law is distinct, with its own set of regulations and practices, so it's imperative to choose a legal advisor who is well-versed in this field. They should possess a deep understanding of franchise-specific issues, which can be critical in navigating the intricacies of franchising agreements and operations.

Experience is another key factor in selecting a franchise attorney. It's wise to opt for an attorney with a wealth of experience in franchising. Such lawyers are likely to have encountered a wide range of franchising scenarios, enabling them to provide informed insights and effective strategies based on their extensive past case histories. Their experience can be invaluable in foreseeing potential issues and providing solutions that are well-grounded in practical realities.

The reputation and references of the attorney also play a significant role. Prospective franchisees or franchisors should research the attorney's standing within the franchising community. Seeking references from other franchisees or franchisors who have worked with the attorney can offer invaluable insights. Positive feedback, word-of-mouth, or testimonials are strong indicators of the attorney's capabilities and reliability. These references can also provide a more personalized perspective on the attorney's approach to handling franchising matters.

Another important aspect is the attorney's ability to understand and align with your business goals and objectives. Every franchise scenario is unique, and it's crucial that the legal advice and services provided are specifically tailored to meet your individual needs and aspirations. This alignment ensures that the legal strategies developed are not only legally sound but also beneficial for the specific goals of your business.

Lastly, accessibility and effective communication are key qualities to look for in a franchise attorney. The franchising world often involves time-sensitive decisions and complex legal procedures. Therefore, it is essential to have an advisor who is not only responsive but also capable of explaining intricate legal concepts in clear, understandable language. An attorney who is readily accessible and communicates effectively can be a significant asset, ensuring that you're well-informed and able to make timely decisions throughout your franchising journey.

How Legal Advisors Can Help

Legal advisors assist in various aspects of franchising, from the initial stages of agreement drafting to ongoing compliance and dispute resolution. Their assistance can be broken down into several key areas:

Reviewing and Drafting Franchise Agreements: Attorneys review and draft franchise agreements, ensuring they are fair, comply with legal standards, and protect the client's interests. They help in understanding the implications of each clause, from territory rights to renewal and termination policies.

Negotiating Terms: Legal advisors play a crucial role in negotiating the terms of franchise agreements. They can advocate for terms that are more favorable to their clients, whether it's lower upfront fees, more territorial exclusivity, or more favorable renewal terms.

Compliance with Laws and Regulations: Attorneys ensure that franchisors and franchisees comply with relevant laws and regulations. This includes adhering to the FTC's franchising rules, state-specific franchise registration and disclosure requirements, and other pertinent business laws. They help in preparing and reviewing the Franchise Disclosure Document (FDD), a critical element in the franchising process, ensuring it's comprehensive and compliant.

Protecting Intellectual Property: For franchisors, protecting their brand and intellectual property is paramount. Legal advisors help in structuring agreements and policies that safeguard trademarks, trade secrets, and proprietary systems.

Conflict Resolution and Litigation: Franchise relationships, like any business relationships, can face conflicts. Legal advisors assist in resolving disputes through negotiation, mediation, or arbitration, and represent clients in litigation if necessary. Their expertise is vital in finding solutions that protect their clients' interests while maintaining business relationships where possible.

Advising on Expansion and Growth Strategies: For franchisors looking to expand, legal advisors provide guidance on growth strategies, including structuring multi-unit franchising, area development agreements, and master franchising. They can also assist in international franchising, navigating the complexities of different countries' franchising laws.

Assistance with Renewals and Transfers: Legal advisors aid in the process of franchise renewals and transfers. They help in understanding and negotiating renewal terms, ensuring continuity for the franchisee. In transfers, they assist in vetting potential buyers and ensuring the transfer process complies with the franchise agreement and applicable laws.

Ongoing Legal Support and Advice: Beyond the initial stages of franchising, legal advisors provide ongoing support. They keep clients updated on changes in franchising laws and regulations, advise on operational legal matters, and assist in strategic decision-making.

In conclusion, the role of legal advisors in franchising is multifaceted and crucial. They provide the expertise necessary to navigate the complex legal landscape of franchising, ensuring that agreements are fair, compliant, and aligned with clients' business goals. Selecting the right legal advisor, one who is experienced, specialized in franchising, and aligned with your business objectives, is a critical step in establishing a successful franchise. Their involvement can make the difference between a thriving franchise relationship and a fraught one, marked by legal pitfalls and missed opportunities. Whether you are a new franchisee or an established franchisor, the value of a competent legal advisor cannot be overstated in the franchising world.

Navigating Franchise Regulations and Compliance

Franchising, as a business model, is subject to a range of regulations at the federal, state, and local levels. Understanding and complying with these laws is crucial for both franchisors and franchisees to operate legally and successfully. This section explores the landscape of franchise regulations and the critical role of the Franchise Disclosure Document (FDD), along with the importance of local compliance.

At the federal level, the primary regulation governing franchising is the Federal Trade Commission (FTC) Rule on Franchising. This rule mandates franchisors to provide potential franchisees with all the information necessary to make an informed decision about their investment. Key requirements include the disclosure of 23 specific items about the franchise, its officers, and other franchisees.

The FTC Rule aims to ensure transparency and prevent deceptive practices in the sale of franchises. It requires the delivery of the Franchise Disclosure Document (FDD) to the prospective franchisee at least 14 days before any agreement is signed or any payment is made.

State laws regarding franchising vary and can often be more stringent than federal regulations. Some states require franchisors to register their FDDs with a state regulatory agency before they can offer or sell franchises within that state. These states are known as "registration states" and include California, Maryland, and New York, among others.

Other states have "relationship laws" that govern the franchise relationship, covering areas such as the renewal, termination, and transfer of franchise agreements. These laws are designed to protect franchisees from unfair practices by franchisors.

Franchise Disclosure Document (FDD)

The FDD is a comprehensive document that provides essential information about the franchisor, the franchise system, and the terms of the franchise agreement. The importance of the FDD in the franchising process cannot be overstated. It includes:

- **Background of the Franchisor:** Information about the franchisor's history, business experience, and executive team.

- **Initial and Ongoing Costs:** Details of the initial franchise fee, ongoing royalty fees, advertising fees, and other potential costs associated with starting and operating the franchise.

- **Franchisee Obligations:** Outline of the franchisee's responsibilities under the franchise agreement.

* * *

- **Restrictions on Goods and Services:** Any restrictions on the goods or services the franchisee may sell.

- **Territorial Rights:** Information on territorial rights and exclusivity, if applicable.

- **Renewal, Termination, and Transfer Policies:** Terms outlining how the franchise relationship can be renewed, terminated, or transferred.

- **Litigation and Bankruptcy History:** Disclosure of any relevant litigation or bankruptcy involving the franchisor or its executives.

- **Financial Performance Representations:** If provided, this includes earnings claims or financial performance data to help potential franchisees assess profitability.

- **List of Current and Former Franchisees:** Contact information for existing and former franchisees, which can be a valuable resource for prospective franchisees to gather insights.

The FDD is crucial for due diligence. Prospective franchisees are advised to thoroughly review the FDD, ask questions, and consider seeking advice from legal and financial advisors experienced in franchising.

Compliance with Local Laws and Ordinances

In addition to federal and state regulations, franchisors and franchisees must comply with local laws and ordinances. These may include business licenses, health and safety codes, employment laws, and zoning regulations. Local laws can vary significantly from one jurisdiction to another and can have a substantial impact on how a franchise operates.

For example, a franchise in the food service industry must adhere to local health department regulations, which can vary widely in terms of food handling, safety standards, and inspection processes. Similarly, local employment laws can dictate wage levels, employee benefits, and working conditions.

Franchisees must ensure they are aware of and comply with these local requirements. Non-compliance can result in fines, legal action, and in severe cases, the closure of the business. It's important for franchisees to engage with local authorities, understand their obligations, and stay informed about any changes in local laws that may affect their business.

Navigating the maze of franchise regulations and compliance is a critical aspect of successful franchising. Understanding and adhering to federal and state franchise laws, thoroughly reviewing and comprehending the FDD, and being compliant with local laws and ordinances are foundational steps in building a sustainable franchise business.

Both franchisors and franchisees must recognize the importance of these regulations not only as legal requirements but as tools to ensure fair practices, transparency, and informed decision-making in the franchising process. Compliance not only protects the franchise system but also enhances its reputation and operational efficiency, leading to long-term success and growth.

Franchise Contract Negotiation and Customization

Entering into a franchise agreement is a nuanced process that requires careful negotiation and possible customization. This journey begins with a comprehensive understanding of the franchisor's position, as they aim to maintain brand consistency and quality across all locations. To effectively negotiate, it's essential to conduct thorough research on the franchise system, which includes understanding financial requirements, operational standards, and the performance of existing franchises. This research forms the backbone of your negotiation strategy, empowering you with knowledge and confidence.

* * *

Negotiating a franchise agreement is not about winning every point but identifying which terms offer room for flexibility. Typically, aspects like territory rights, initial fees, or aspects of training support may be open to discussion. It's crucial to engage with a franchise attorney or a financial advisor specializing in franchising, as their insights can be invaluable in navigating complex contractual terms and suggesting beneficial modifications.

When crafting your negotiation strategy, it's important to prioritize the terms most crucial for your business's success while being prepared to compromise on less critical aspects. Effective negotiation involves finding a balance that satisfies both your business goals and the franchisor's need for uniformity. Clear, concise, and professional communication is key during these discussions, ensuring that your concerns and suggestions are understood and considered.

Customization of a franchise agreement is possible but within certain boundaries. Franchisors seek uniformity in their franchise system, which limits the extent of customization. However, modifications can be made to suit local market conditions or based on your unique skills and business goals. For example, leveraging your strong marketing background could be a basis for negotiating more autonomy in local advertising strategies. Similarly, adaptations to meet local market tastes and regulations can be critical for the franchise's success and may be negotiable if backed by solid market research and data.

Negotiating the renewal terms of the franchise agreement is often overlooked but can be crucial for long-term planning. Any modifications agreed upon should be thoroughly documented in writing, as verbal agreements can lead to misunderstandings and disputes. After negotiations and any customizations are made, it's vital to review the agreement meticulously, ideally with legal assistance, to ensure all terms are accurately reflected and understood.

In summary, negotiating and customizing a franchise contract is a critical and intricate process that lays the groundwork for a successful franchise relationship. It requires a strategic approach, an understanding of the franchisor's business model, and an ability to propose reasonable modifications. By preparing thoroughly, understanding the franchisor's perspective, and seeking expert advice, franchisees can negotiate terms that align more closely with their individual needs and goals, ultimately leading to a prosperous and mutually beneficial partnership.

Case Studies and Real-World Examples

Successful Negotiation Strategies

Case Study 1: The Coffee Shop Franchisee

John, an aspiring entrepreneur, was interested in opening a franchise of a popular coffee shop brand. During the negotiation of the franchise agreement, John noticed that the proposed territory for his outlet was quite expansive, but it included an area already saturated with coffee shops. Using his local market knowledge, he successfully negotiated a smaller, more focused territory with less competition, arguing it would benefit both parties through higher sales and brand visibility. John's case exemplifies the importance of understanding local market conditions and using this knowledge to negotiate a franchise agreement that maximizes potential for success.

Case Study 2: The Fast-Food Franchise Renewal

Sarah, an experienced franchisee of a fast-food chain, was approaching the renewal of her franchise agreement. She used her strong performance and compliance history as leverage in her negotiations. Sarah proposed a reduction in ongoing royalty fees, citing her outlet's contribution to the brand's reputation and consistent revenue generation. The franchisor, recognizing her value and wanting to retain a successful franchisee, agreed to a reduced rate. This case highlights how a franchisee's proven track record can be a powerful tool in negotiating more favorable terms, especially when it comes to renewals.

Case Study 3: Dispute Over Territory Rights

Alex, a franchisee of a home services brand, faced a legal challenge when the franchisor granted another franchisee rights to operate in an overlapping territory. Alex had assumed his territory rights were exclusive based on initial discussions, but the written agreement was ambiguous on this point. The dispute escalated to legal proceedings. Ultimately, the court favored Alex, citing the principle of good faith and fair dealing in franchise relationships. This ruling forced the franchisor to adjust the territories. This case underscores the importance of ensuring all verbal agreements are clearly articulated and documented in the franchise agreement to avoid costly legal disputes.

Case Study 4: Resolving Non-Compliance Issues

Linda, a retail franchisee, faced legal challenges when the franchisor accused her of non-compliance with brand guidelines. The franchisor threatened termination of the franchise agreement. However, Linda sought legal counsel and was able to demonstrate that the alleged non-compliance issues were based on newly introduced standards that hadn't been properly communicated to her. The resolution involved Linda agreeing to adhere to the new standards while the franchisor committed to better communication of any future changes. This case illustrates the potential for misunderstandings in franchise operations and the importance of open communication and legal guidance in resolving compliance disputes.

These case studies highlight various aspects of franchise contract negotiations and legal challenges. John's and Sarah's stories emphasize the importance of leveraging market knowledge and performance history in negotiations, while Alex's and Linda's experiences illustrate the crucial role of clear communication and legal assistance in resolving disputes. Together, they provide valuable insights for prospective franchisees into the complexities of franchising and the strategies that can lead to successful outcomes.

Conclusion

* * *

In summarizing the key legal and contractual aspects of franchising, we recognize the intricate balance between entrepreneurial ambition and the necessity of stringent compliance with a set of complex legalities. The journey through franchising is marked by a deep dive into franchise agreements, where understanding terms like fees, territory rights, and operational standards becomes crucial. Additionally, the negotiation and potential customization of these agreements open avenues for tailoring a franchise to specific needs, albeit within the confines of brand consistency and legal frameworks.

The role of legal advisors in this process cannot be overstated. They are the navigators in the choppy waters of franchise law, guiding both franchisors and franchisees through the intricacies of agreements, compliance, and potential disputes. Moreover, the real-world examples and case studies discussed illustrate the practical application of these legal principles, offering insights into successful strategies and resolutions of common challenges.

Understanding and carefully considering these legal and contractual aspects is not merely a recommendation but a necessity for anyone embarking on a franchising journey. It's about making informed decisions that align with personal business goals while maintaining the integrity and standards of the franchising model.

Additional Resources

For further reading and research, the following resources are invaluable for deepening one's understanding of franchising law:

Books:

"Franchise Law for Dummies" by Michael H. Seid and Dave Thomas
"Franchising For Dummies" by Michael Seid and Joyce Mazero
"The Franchisee Handbook" by Mark Siebert

Websites:

* * *

International Franchise Association (IFA): www.franchise.org
American Bar Association Forum on Franchising:
www.americanbar.org/groups/franchising
Franchise Direct: www.franchisedirect.com

Legal Advisors and Firms Specializing in Franchising:

DLA Piper Global Franchise Group: Offers comprehensive services in franchise law globally.
Gray Plant Mooty: Known for their expertise in franchise and distribution law.
Nixon Peabody LLP: Offers a range of services including franchising, distribution, and brand development.

This chapter is designed to equip potential franchisees with the knowledge needed to navigate the complex legal terrain of franchising. By understanding these crucial aspects, franchisees can embark on this path with confidence, backed by the power of informed decision-making and the support of specialized legal expertise.

CHAPTER FIVE

PREPARING FOR FRANCHISE OWNERSHIP

Embarking on the journey of franchise ownership is an exciting venture, yet one that requires meticulous preparation and strategic planning. This chapter is dedicated to emphasizing the significance of this preparation, outlining the critical steps and considerations for potential franchise owners. It serves as a comprehensive guide, illuminating the path from the initial conception of owning a franchise to the successful operation of one.

Understanding the landscape of franchise ownership extends beyond just the financial investment; it involves a deep dive into the development of a robust business plan tailored to the specificities of the franchise model. This plan is the foundation upon which a successful franchise is built, encompassing detailed financial projections, thorough market analysis, and strategic operational plans. It's a tool that not only guides the franchisee but also aligns their vision with the franchisor's established business model and objectives.

Moreover, the chapter delves into the critical aspects of training and support provided by franchisors. This support is a cornerstone of franchise success, offering guidance, resources, and expertise to navigate the initial setup and ongoing operations. We explore how leveraging this support effectively can accelerate the growth and stability of the franchise.

The process of setting up the franchise also takes center stage, with a focus on selecting the optimal location, staffing efficiently, and implementing operational workflows that adhere to the franchisor's guidelines. These initial steps are pivotal in establishing a franchise that resonates with the target market and operates seamlessly.

Lastly, the chapter addresses the vital role of marketing and branding for new franchisees. It underscores the importance of adhering to the franchisor's brand guidelines while employing innovative marketing strategies to capture and engage the local market. From digital marketing to community involvement, these strategies are instrumental in carving a niche for the franchise in a competitive landscape.

In essence, this chapter is crafted to provide potential franchisees with a thorough understanding of what it takes to prepare for franchise ownership. It's a roadmap for transforming the dream of owning a franchise into a reality, equipped with informed strategies, practical insights, and a clear vision for success.

Developing a Business Plan for Your Franchise

Entering the world of franchising demands not only a financial investment but also a strategic and well-structured business plan. This plan is a roadmap that guides the franchisee through the complexities of operating a franchise successfully. In this chapter, we explore the essential components of a franchise business plan and the strategies to align it with the franchisor's model while setting realistic goals for growth and expansion.

The success of any franchise heavily relies on the foundation laid out by a comprehensive and tailored business plan. This plan serves multiple functions: it provides a clear vision and direction, helps in securing financing, and serves as a tool for ongoing business management. For a franchise, a business plan must be customized to fit the specific requirements and guidelines of the franchisor while also considering the unique aspects of the local market where the franchise will operate.

* * *

Essential Elements of a Franchise Business Plan

Executive Summary: This section provides an overview of the business, including the franchise's concept, the business model, ownership structure, and a brief description of products or services offered. It should capture the essence of what the franchise stands for and its value proposition.

Franchise Model Analysis: This part of the plan delves into the specifics of the franchisor's model. It should outline the franchisor's history, the success of their model, support systems in place, and any unique selling points that set this franchise apart from competitors.

Market Analysis: A comprehensive market analysis is crucial. This includes researching the local market, understanding target demographics, analyzing competitors, and identifying market trends. This section should demonstrate that there is a demand for the franchise's products or services in the intended area.

Marketing and Sales Strategies: Detailing how the franchise intends to attract and retain customers is vital. This section should align with the franchisor's overall marketing strategy but also include local tactics. It must cover advertising, promotions, digital marketing strategies, and sales tactics tailored to the local market.

Financial Projections: One of the most critical elements of the plan, this section should provide detailed financial forecasts, including startup costs, ongoing operational expenses, revenue projections, and break-even analysis. These projections should be realistic, based on thorough market research and the franchisor's historical data.

Operational Strategies: This part should detail the day-to-day operations of the franchise, including staffing, management processes, customer service protocols, inventory management, and supplier relations. Operational plans should align with the franchisor's standards to ensure consistency and efficiency.

Location Analysis: For franchises where location is key, this section should justify the chosen site. It should include details on foot traffic, accessibility, local demographics, and how the location fits within the broader market strategy.

Aligning with the Franchisor's Established Business Model

Aligning the business plan with the franchisor's model is fundamental for franchise success. Franchisors provide a proven business model, including brand guidelines, operational procedures, and marketing strategies. The business plan should reflect a deep understanding of this model and demonstrate how the franchisee will replicate this success in their local market. This alignment ensures that the franchise operates under the successful umbrella of the franchisor while tailoring certain aspects to fit the specific market needs.

Setting realistic goals is essential in the business planning process. These goals should be specific, measurable, achievable, relevant, and time-bound (SMART). Objectives should include short-term and long-term financial targets, customer growth metrics, market expansion plans, and benchmarks for operational efficiency. These goals should be ambitious yet attainable, considering both the franchisor's track record and the specific market dynamics.

Short-Term Goals: These might include launching the franchise successfully, reaching a certain revenue target in the first year, establishing a strong customer base, or achieving operational efficiency.

Long-Term Goals: Long-term objectives could encompass expanding to additional locations, becoming a market leader in the region, or diversifying the product or service offerings as per market demands.

Continuous Assessment and Adaptation: The business plan should be a living document, open to adjustments and changes based on market feedback and operational experiences. Regular review and adaptation of the plan ensure that the franchise remains on track to meet its objectives.

* * *

In conclusion, a well-developed business plan is a cornerstone of franchise success. It acts as a blueprint guiding the franchisee through the complex journey of franchising. By thoroughly understanding the franchisor's business model, conducting in-depth market analysis, and setting realistic goals, a franchisee can create a business plan that not only aligns with the franchisor's vision but also caters to the nuances of the local market. Such a plan not only facilitates a strong start but also supports sustained growth and expansion, ensuring the long-term success and profitability of the franchise. Aspiring franchise owners should approach this task with diligence, research, and foresight, laying the groundwork for a thriving enterprise that resonates with customers and stands the test of time in a competitive business landscape.

Training and Support: Leveraging Franchisor Expertise

For franchisees, one of the most significant advantages of entering into a franchise agreement is the access to extensive training and support from the franchisor. This chapter delves into the various training programs offered by franchisors, the critical role of ongoing support, strategies to maximize these benefits, and real-world examples that highlight the impact of effective training and support on franchisee success.

Franchisors typically offer comprehensive training programs designed to equip franchisees with the knowledge and skills needed to operate their franchise successfully. These programs often cover a wide range of topics, including:

- Operational Training: This includes hands-on training in managing day-to-day operations, understanding the franchisor's systems and processes, and adhering to operational standards.

- Financial Management Training: Franchisees are trained in

financial record-keeping, budgeting, and managing cash flow, which are crucial for the financial health of the franchise.

- Sales and Customer Service Training: Since the brand's reputation heavily relies on customer experience, franchisors often provide extensive training in sales techniques and customer service best practices.

- Product or Service Specific Training: Detailed training on the specific products or services offered by the franchise, including preparation, presentation, and quality control.

- Compliance Training: Ensuring that franchisees understand and comply with legal requirements, health and safety standards, and employment laws.

The Importance of Ongoing Support from the Franchisor

The sustained success of a franchise hinges not only on the initial training provided by the franchisor but also on the continuous support that follows. This ongoing support from the franchisor is a multifaceted engagement, vital for the franchisee's long-term growth and adaptation to evolving business environments.

One of the key aspects of this support is operational guidance. Franchisors offer continuous advice on daily operations, introduce new products, and suggest process improvements. This kind of support ensures that franchisees stay abreast of the latest operational strategies and are able to maintain efficiency and effectiveness in their business practices.

Equally important is the support in marketing and branding. Franchisors assist franchisees in implementing effective marketing strategies, provide access to national advertising campaigns, and offer guidance on local marketing efforts. This support is crucial in maintaining brand consistency and maximizing the franchise's visibility and appeal in various markets.

* * *

Franchisors also play a pivotal role in keeping franchisees updated with the latest industry trends, technological advancements, and innovative practices. This regular influx of new information and ideas helps franchisees stay competitive and adapt to changing market demands.

Another significant facet of franchisor support is troubleshooting and problem-solving. Franchisors provide solutions and support to help franchisees overcome various business challenges that may arise, ensuring the smooth operation and resilience of the franchise.

To maximize the benefits of the training and support offered by franchisors, franchisees should adopt several strategies

. Engaging actively in training programs is essential. Franchisees should participate fully in all training sessions, asking questions and seeking clarity on any aspects they are unsure about. This proactive engagement fosters a deeper understanding of the business and its operations.

Applying the concepts learned during training is equally crucial. The practical application of skills and knowledge in day-to-day operations is where the real value of training manifests. By diligently implementing these learned concepts, franchisees can enhance their business proficiency and effectiveness.

Maintaining open communication with the franchisor is also key. Regular interactions help franchisees stay informed about any changes within the franchise system and provide a channel to seek assistance when needed. This open line of communication ensures that franchisees are always in sync with the franchisor's latest policies and strategies.

Networking opportunities provided by the franchisor can be highly beneficial. Many franchisors create platforms for franchisees to network, share experiences, and learn from each other. Engaging in these networks can offer valuable insights

, peer support, and the chance to learn from the successes and challenges of fellow franchisees.

Lastly, it's vital for franchisees to utilize the marketing and branding resources provided by the franchisor effectively. These tools and guidelines are designed to ensure consistency in branding and effectiveness in promotional efforts. By leveraging these resources, franchisees can enhance their market presence and align their local marketing strategies with the broader goals of the franchise brand.

In summary, the ongoing support from the franchisor is an invaluable asset for franchisees. It encompasses operational guidance, marketing and branding support, regular updates on industry trends, and assistance in troubleshooting. By actively engaging in training programs, applying learned concepts, maintaining open communication, leveraging networking opportunities, and utilizing marketing resources, franchisees can maximize the benefits of this support, leading to sustained success and growth in their franchising venture.

Real-World Examples Illustrating the Impact of Effective Training and Support

Example of a Fast-Food Franchise: A Wendy's franchisee in Buffalo, NY attributed their success to the comprehensive operational training received, which included specific product preparation techniques and customer service standards. The franchisor's ongoing operational support helped them adapt to changing consumer preferences and maintain high standards.

Success in a Retail Franchise: A Target franchisee in Hampton, VA leveraged the franchisor's marketing support to launch targeted local marketing campaigns, in addition to participating in national promotions. This dual approach significantly increased foot traffic and sales at their location.

Technology Integration in a Service Franchise: A RE/MAX franchisee in New Haven, CT effectively implemented new technology and systems as part of the franchisor's innovation training. This adoption not only streamlined operations but also improved service delivery and customer satisfaction.

These examples underscore the transformative impact that franchisor-provided training and support can have on a franchise's operations and success. By fully embracing and utilizing these resources, franchisees can enhance their business's performance, adapt to market changes, and sustain growth over time. This chapter emphasizes that while the franchisor's expertise and support are invaluable assets, the franchisee's commitment to learning and applying these insights is equally critical for achieving success in the franchising venture.

Setting Up Your Franchise: Location, Staffing, and Operations

Setting up a franchise is a multifaceted endeavor, involving critical decisions about location, staffing, and operational strategies. Each element plays a crucial role in the franchise's overall success and must align with the franchisor's guidelines and market demands. This chapter delves into the intricacies of these components, offering practical guidance, relevant facts, figures, and real-world examples.

The adage "location, location, location" holds particularly true in franchising. The choice of location can significantly influence a franchise's foot traffic, revenue, and market penetration. According to a report by the International Franchise Association, about 33% of franchisees consider location as one of their top three challenges.

1. Franchisor Criteria: Franchisors typically have specific criteria for location selection, based on their experience and market research. This may include demographic factors, foot traffic, visibility, accessibility, and proximity to complementary businesses. It's crucial to understand and adhere to these criteria to benefit from the franchisor's proven model.

2. **Market Research:** Conducting local market research is imperative. This includes analyzing the area's demographic profile, consumer behavior, competition density, and economic

conditions. For instance, a quick-service restaurant franchise would thrive in a location with high foot traffic and a younger demographic.

3. **Real Estate Considerations:** Evaluate the cost of leasing or purchasing property, zoning laws, and potential for growth. For example, a study by JLL Retail revealed that retail franchises often prefer locations in high-traffic urban centers or popular malls.

Determining Staffing Needs

Staffing is a crucial element in the successful establishment of a franchise, significantly impacting customer experience, sales, and the overall reputation of the brand.

The process begins with assessing staff requirements, which varies depending on the franchise model. For example, a retail franchise might need a team of sales associates, while a service-based franchise could require skilled technicians. The key is to determine the number and type of staff needed to ensure efficient and effective operations.

Once the staffing needs are identified, the next step is implementing hiring strategies that align with the franchise's culture and values. This might involve utilizing online job portals, tapping into local employment agencies, or leveraging resources provided by the franchisor. The aim is to recruit individuals who not only possess the necessary skills but also fit well with the franchise's ethos and work culture.

Training programs play an integral role in preparing the staff to meet the franchise's standards. According to the National Franchise Institute, effective training can significantly enhance employee retention, by up to 50%. Franchisors typically provide training programs, but it's also beneficial to incorporate additional training tailored to specific operational needs. This ensures that staff members are well-versed in the brand's protocols and are equipped to uphold its reputation through excellent service.

* * *

Setting up operations for a franchise involves a meticulous process that requires alignment with franchisor guidelines while adapting to local market conditions. Developing an efficient operational workflow is crucial. This includes setting up point-of-sale systems, establishing customer service protocols, and organizing back-office operations. Compliance with the franchisor's operational standards is non-negotiable, especially in franchises with strict industry regulations, like those in the food industry that require adherence to specific health and safety standards.

Integrating technology is a key factor in operational efficiency. Incorporating systems like franchise management software can streamline various functions, including inventory management, scheduling, and sales tracking, thus enhancing overall operational effectiveness.

Inventory management and a reliable supply chain are fundamental for the smooth running of a franchise. Implementing an effective inventory control system is essential. This system should align with the franchisor's guidelines and be tailored to meet the specific needs of the business. It should accurately monitor stock levels, order times, and sales patterns to minimize the risks of stockouts and overstocking. The National Retail Federation has indicated that effective inventory management is crucial, as retailers can lose billions due to either excess inventory or lack of stock.

Building strong relationships with approved suppliers is another vital aspect of running a successful franchise. Adhering to the franchisor's supply chain policies is key to maintaining product consistency and quality. For instance, a fast-food franchise must source ingredients exclusively from approved suppliers to ensure uniformity in taste and quality across all locations.

Efficiency in supply chain management can lead to significant cost savings and operational improvements. Franchisees should aim to negotiate favorable terms with suppliers and consider local sourcing options to reduce costs where appropriate. A well-organized supply chain is not just about cost management; it's about ensuring the timely availability of products and services. For example, McDonald's is known for its highly efficient supply chain strategy, saving the company an estimated $750 million annually.

Incorporating technology in supply chain management is increasingly important. Using inventory management software can automate ordering processes, track sales trends, and accurately forecast future inventory needs. This technological integration reduces the risk of human error and inefficiency, leading to a more streamlined operation. A notable example is Subway, which utilizes a sophisticated supply chain management system for real-time inventory tracking and automatic reordering, maintaining optimal stock levels across its franchises.

In summary, the right team, effective training, operational efficiency, and robust inventory and supply chain management are pivotal for the success of a franchise. These elements collectively enhance the customer experience, drive sales, and uphold the franchise's brand reputation, contributing significantly to the overall success of the franchise business.

Real-World Examples and Best Practices

Starbucks' Location Strategy: Starbucks' success can partly be attributed to its strategic location choices, often placing stores in high-traffic areas and corners visible from multiple directions. They use sophisticated mapping and data analytics to choose locations that align with their target market's lifestyle.

Chick-fil-A's Staffing and Training: Chick-fil-A is renowned for its customer service, largely due to its rigorous staffing and training processes. The company invests heavily in employee training, focusing on customer interaction and operational efficiency, which has contributed to its high customer satisfaction ratings.

Walmart's Supply Chain Efficiency: Walmart's supply chain efficiency is a benchmark in retail franchising. They use an advanced and integrated supply chain management system, which includes vendor-managed inventory, resulting in reduced inventory costs and improved in-stock rates.

In conclusion, setting up a franchise involves critical decisions regarding location, staffing, and operations, each requiring a strategic approach and alignment with the franchisor's guidelines. By choosing the right location, employing and training the right staff, and establishing efficient operational and inventory management systems, franchisees can position their businesses for success. The integration of technology and adherence to best practices, as demonstrated by successful franchises, further enhances the potential for growth and profitability in the competitive world of franchising.

Marketing and Branding Strategies for New Franchisees

In the bustling world of franchising, the art of marketing and branding takes on a unique flavor, balancing franchisor guidelines with local market nuances. For new franchisees, navigating this landscape is akin to choreographing a dance that honors the franchisor's established brand while infusing local flair and relevance.

At the heart of a franchise's marketing strategy lies the necessity to adhere to the franchisor's brand guidelines. These guidelines are the franchise's North Star, ensuring that no matter where a customer interacts with the brand, be it in a bustling city or a quiet suburb, the experience remains consistent. This consistency is crucial for building brand trust and recognition. For instance, when you walk into a McDonald's, whether it's in New York or Tokyo, there's a comforting familiarity in the brand experience, from the menu items down to the logo and color scheme.

For new franchisees, understanding and embracing these guidelines should be the first step in their marketing journey. The franchisor usually provides a comprehensive branding manual that covers everything from logo usage, color schemes, to the tone of voice for communications. This uniformity in branding is what allows franchises like Starbucks or Subway to maintain a cohesive brand image globally. It's not just about logos and colors; it's about conveying a consistent brand message and experience.

Developing Local Market Strategies

While adhering to national brand standards, franchisees also need to tailor their marketing strategies to fit local market dynamics. This local adaptation is where the franchisee's intimate knowledge of their community becomes invaluable. For example, a Dunkin' Donuts in a college town might focus on promotions around exam seasons, while one in a corporate area might offer breakfast meeting packages.

This localization involves understanding the unique needs and preferences of the local audience and then customizing marketing efforts to address them. It's about finding that sweet spot where the national brand message resonates with local interests and trends. For instance, a gym franchise in a family-oriented neighborhood might offer parent-child fitness classes, aligning with the community's values while staying true to the brand's fitness focus.

Leveraging Digital Marketing and Social Media

In today's digital age, online presence is crucial for any business, and franchises are no exception. Digital marketing and social media offer powerful tools for franchisees to enhance local brand visibility and engagement. Platforms like Facebook, Instagram, and Google My Business allow franchisees to target local audiences effectively.

Social media, in particular, offers an opportunity for franchisees to humanize their brand and engage directly with their community. For example, a local pizza franchise can use Instagram to showcase their participation in community events or run Facebook ads targeting pizza lovers in their vicinity. These platforms also provide valuable insights into customer preferences and behaviors, enabling franchisees to refine their marketing strategies continuously.

Moreover, leveraging the franchisor's national online campaigns can amplify the local franchise's visibility. By participating in national social media challenges or promotions, local franchises can tap into a broader audience while maintaining their local relevance.

Building a Local Presence Through Community Involvement

Perhaps one of the most impactful marketing strategies for new franchisees is building a strong local presence through community involvement and networking. This approach goes beyond traditional advertising and delves into forming genuine connections within the community. Engaging in local events, sponsoring school sports teams, or participating in charity fundraisers are ways a franchise can embed itself into the local fabric.

This community-focused approach not only raises brand awareness but also builds goodwill and loyalty among local residents. For instance, a coffee shop franchise that hosts local art exhibitions or open mic nights becomes more than just a place to get coffee; it transforms into a community hub, a place where connections are made, and loyalty is built.

Networking is another crucial aspect of local marketing. Joining local business associations, chambers of commerce, or networking groups can open doors to collaborations, partnerships, and new customer segments. It's an opportunity to learn from other local businesses and share experiences.

Case Studies and Best Practices

Real-world examples abound of franchisees who have successfully leveraged these strategies. A notable case is that of a Subway franchise in a small town that organized and sponsored a local youth baseball tournament. The event not only provided exposure to the brand but also established the franchise as a community-centric business, leading to increased patronage and loyalty.

* * *

Another example is a retail franchise that optimized its local SEO strategies, ensuring that they appeared in local search results, which significantly increased foot traffic to their store. They complemented this with a strong social media presence, showcasing their involvement in local events and causes, which resonated well with the community.

Marketing and branding for new franchisees involve a delicate balance between adhering to franchisor guidelines and adapting to local market dynamics. By embracing the franchisor's brand guidelines, tailoring marketing strategies to the local audience, leveraging digital platforms, and actively participating in the community, franchisees can effectively build brand presence and loyalty. These strategies, combined with real-life examples and best practices, offer a blueprint for franchisees aiming to carve out their niche in the competitive world of franchising and drive their business towards growth and success.

Conclusion

As we conclude this chapter on preparing for franchise ownership, we reflect on the essential steps and strategies that form the foundation of a successful franchise venture. From the initial stages of developing a detailed business plan, adhering to the franchisor's brand guidelines, to the intricacies of choosing the right location, staffing appropriately, and setting up efficient operations, each aspect plays a pivotal role in the journey to becoming a successful franchisee.

The journey does not end with setting up the franchise; it extends into effectively marketing and branding the franchise, catering to local market dynamics while staying aligned with national campaigns, and establishing a strong community presence. These facets, when executed well, can significantly enhance the franchise's visibility and appeal to the local customer base. The importance of digital marketing in today's technology-driven world cannot be overstated, offering a powerful platform for franchisees to connect with their audience and build a loyal customer base.

This chapter has emphasized the necessity for potential franchisees to approach franchise ownership with a comprehensive and well-informed strategy. Understanding the full scope of what it takes to launch and sustain a successful franchise is crucial. It requires a blend of adherence to proven systems and creative adaptation to local market needs.

Additional Resources

To further aid in this journey, the following resources are invaluable for anyone looking to deepen their understanding of franchise ownership:

Books

"Franchising For Dummies" by Michael H. Seid and Joyce Mazero: A beginner-friendly guide covering various aspects of franchising.
"The Franchise MBA: Mastering the 4 Essential Steps to Owning a Franchise" by Nick Neonakis: Provides insights into the critical steps in franchise ownership.
"The E-Myth Revisited" by Michael E. Gerber: Although not solely about franchising, this book offers valuable lessons on why most small businesses don't work and what to do about it.

Websites

- International Franchise Association (IFA) - www.franchise.org: A comprehensive resource for franchise opportunities, industry news, and educational materials.
- Franchise Direct - www.franchisedirect.com: Offers a directory of franchise opportunities and a wealth of related articles and guides.
- Entrepreneur's Franchise 500 - www.entrepreneur.com/franchise500: An annual ranking of top franchises with detailed information about each company.

Professional Services and Consulting Firms

FranNet - Provides consulting services to individuals interested in franchising, helping them identify the right opportunity.

The Franchise Consulting Company - Offers guidance through the process of selecting and buying a franchise.

Franchise Business Review - A research firm that provides ratings and reviews of top franchise opportunities based on franchisee satisfaction and performance.

This comprehensive guide aims to empower potential franchisees with the necessary knowledge and tools for a successful launch and sustainable operation of their franchise. The path to successful franchise ownership is multifaceted, demanding careful planning, thorough research, and an adaptable approach. With these resources and a solid understanding of the essentials outlined in this chapter, aspiring franchise owners can navigate their journey with greater confidence and clarity.

CHAPTER SIX

MANAGING YOUR FRANCHISE

In the dynamic world of franchising, the essence of success often lies in effective management. This chapter focuses on the pivotal role that management plays in nurturing the success and ensuring the longevity of a franchise. The journey of a franchise owner is multifaceted, encompassing various domains that require keen attention and strategic execution. The ability to navigate these aspects skillfully is what separates thriving franchises from those that struggle.

As we delve into this chapter, we aim to explore the key components that constitute the backbone of sound franchise management. Each section is designed to provide comprehensive insights and practical guidance on critical areas of franchise operations.

Firstly, we address Financial Management and Budgeting, a cornerstone of any successful business venture. In this section, we'll explore how to create a solid financial foundation, manage revenue and expenses effectively, and utilize financial reports to make informed decisions.

The next focal point is Effective Operational Strategies. This part of the chapter will cover the nuances of streamlining day-to-day operations, adhering to franchisor standards, leveraging technology for efficiency, and managing a robust supply chain.

Understanding the importance of customer relationships, the chapter then transitions to Customer Service Excellence and Community Engagement. Here, we delve into building a customer-centric culture, harnessing feedback for improvement, engaging with the local community, and managing the franchise's reputation.

Growth is an essential aspect of any business, and in the section on Growth and Expansion Opportunities, we will discuss how to identify and capitalize on opportunities for scaling the business, plan strategically for expansion, and assess and mitigate associated risks.

Finally, no business journey is without its hurdles. In Dealing with Challenges and Setbacks, we will examine common challenges faced by franchisees, strategies for effective crisis management, learning from setbacks, and the importance of seeking support when needed.

By understanding and applying the principles and strategies discussed here, franchise owners can enhance their chances of success, create sustainable growth, and navigate the challenges of the business world with confidence and agility. The aim is to empower franchisees with the knowledge and tools necessary to manage their franchise efficiently and effectively, ensuring a robust and prosperous business venture.

Financial Management and Budgeting

In the dynamic and competitive world of franchising, robust financial management emerges as the cornerstone of success. The financial health of a franchise acts as a critical indicator of its operational efficiency and potential for growth. It's this handling of finances, from meticulous budgeting to strategic revenue management, that sets apart thriving franchises.

At the heart of solid financial management lies the art of budgeting. Tailored to the unique demands of the franchise model, a realistic and effective budget is not merely about numbers on a spreadsheet; it's a comprehensive plan that encompasses revenue projections based on historical data and market analysis, and cost estimation that takes into account both fixed and variable expenses. Crucially, it involves astute cash flow management to ensure liquidity for operational needs and future investments, coupled with a contingency plan for unforeseen expenses.

Revenue management in a franchise is a multifaceted endeavor. It requires a blend of astute pricing strategies that balance competitiveness and profitability, innovative sales tactics like promotional offers and loyalty programs, and a drive towards revenue diversification. This diversification, whether through new product launches, online sales channels, or geographic expansion, serves as a hedge against market volatility.

Controlling expenses is another pillar of financial management. Effective expense control involves optimizing inventory levels to reduce costs, efficiently managing staff schedules and training to maximize productivity, and regularly reviewing overhead costs to identify potential savings. This could include adopting energy-efficient practices or negotiating better terms with suppliers.

The role of financial reporting and analysis in a franchise is indispensable. Regular and accurate financial reports such as income statements and balance sheets offer a clear view of the franchise's financial status. These reports should be complemented by a vigilant monitoring of Key Performance Indicators (KPIs) relevant to the franchise's operations. Variance analysis, a critical part of this process, involves comparing actual financial outcomes with the budgeted figures, allowing for timely identification and correction of deviations. This rigorous analysis paves the way for data-driven decision making, crucial in determining strategies for expansion, marketing, and capital investments.

Moreover, benchmarking against industry standards and competitors through these financial analyses can unearth areas for improvement and opportunities for adopting best practices. It's through these practices that a franchise can truly realize its potential.

In summary, the essence of financial management and budgeting in the franchise sphere is not confined to maintaining a balanced ledger. It's about creating a culture of financial discipline and strategic acumen across the franchise network. This involves regular training and development in financial literacy for franchisees and staff, reinforcing a culture that values strategic growth and financial responsibility.

Ultimately, by embedding these financial management and budgeting principles into their operational ethos, franchises can navigate the complexities of the business world, ensuring not just survival but flourishing growth. These principles foster resilience and adaptability, enabling franchises to withstand market fluctuations and seize new opportunities. The journey towards financial mastery in franchising is continuous, demanding consistent evaluation, adaptation, and improvement. Yet, it is this journey that ensures the franchise's long-term success and establishes benchmarks in financial excellence and operational efficiency.

Effective Operational Strategies

Effective operational strategies are the lifeblood of a successful franchise, determining its efficiency, profitability, and ability to scale. At the core of these strategies lies the focus on streamlining operations, aligning with franchisor standards, integrating technology, and managing the supply chain effectively.

Streamlining operations involves implementing best practices that enhance the efficiency of franchise operations. This encompasses efficient inventory management, where the goal is to maintain optimal stock levels to meet demand without overstocking or understocking. Workflow optimization is another critical area, requiring a close look at how tasks and processes are executed and finding ways to make them more efficient. This could involve reorganizing the workspace, adopting lean management techniques, or refining employee roles and responsibilities for better productivity.

Compliance with franchisor standards is critical for maintaining the integrity and reputation of the franchise brand. Franchises need to align their operations with the guidelines and quality standards set by the franchisor. This ensures consistency in customer experience across different locations, which is crucial for building customer trust and loyalty. Regular training and audits can help in maintaining these standards, ensuring that every aspect of the franchise's operations, from customer service to product presentation, adheres to the franchisor's expectations.

Technology integration plays a transformative role in modern franchise operations. Leveraging technology and software for operational efficiency is no longer a luxury but a necessity. Point of Sale (POS) systems, for instance, can streamline transactions, inventory tracking, and sales reporting. Advanced inventory management tools can automate ordering processes, track stock levels in real-time, and predict inventory needs based on sales trends. Implementing such technologies not only boosts efficiency but also provides valuable data insights for informed decision-making.

Supply chain management is a critical aspect that franchises must master to ensure the smooth running of operations. Effective supply chain strategies are essential for maintaining product quality and achieving cost-effectiveness. This involves establishing strong relationships with suppliers, negotiating favorable terms, and ensuring a reliable and efficient logistics network. Moreover, franchises must be agile in their supply chain strategies to respond to market changes, supplier issues, or logistical challenges promptly.

In conclusion, effective operational strategies in franchising hinge on four pillars: streamlining operations for maximum efficiency, adhering strictly to franchisor standards to maintain brand integrity, integrating cutting-edge technology for operational excellence, and managing a robust supply chain for quality and cost-effectiveness. Mastery of these areas not only contributes to the smooth running of daily operations but also sets the foundation for sustainable growth and competitive advantage in the franchise industry.

Customer Service Excellence and Community Engagement

By building a customer-centric culture, actively utilizing customer feedback, engaging with the local community, and managing the brand's reputation effectively, businesses can establish a lasting bond with their customers and the community at large. This will enhance your brand's reputation in the local community, and will likely lead to an increase in business.

Creating a customer-centric culture involves ingraining a strong service ethic among staff and management. This transformation begins with leadership that not only preaches the importance of customer service but also leads by example. Training programs should be implemented to educate employees on the value of customer satisfaction and the techniques to achieve it. Regular workshops and team-building activities can reinforce this ethos, making customer service a core part of the company's identity. Employees should be encouraged to understand the customer's perspective and empowered to make decisions that enhance the customer experience. Recognizing and rewarding staff for exceptional customer service further motivates them to uphold these standards.

Customer feedback is a goldmine of information, offering insights into what a business is doing right and what needs improvement. Actively seeking out and utilizing this feedback is crucial for refining service offerings and enhancing customer satisfaction. This can be achieved through surveys, comment cards, or digital platforms. It is important to analyze this feedback comprehensively and implement changes based on it. Responding to customer feedback, especially when it points out flaws or suggests improvements, demonstrates a business's commitment to its customers and can turn negative experiences into positive ones.

Engaging with the local community goes a long way in building brand loyalty and a positive corporate image. This can be achieved through hosting and participating in community events, sponsorships of local teams or causes, and forming partnerships with other local businesses or non-profits. Community involvement should align with the business's values and aim to genuinely contribute to the community. This not only helps in building a loyal customer base but also establishes the business as a responsible and integral part of the community.

In the digital age, online reviews and social media play a significant role in shaping a brand's reputation. Handling customer complaints and managing online reviews is a delicate but essential part of reputation management. It's important to address complaints promptly and effectively, ensuring that the customer feels heard and valued. Responses to negative reviews should be professional, empathetic, and solution-oriented. Proactively managing a positive online presence, through regular updates and engagement with customers on social media platforms, can significantly enhance a brand's image.

Customer service excellence and community engagement are critical aspects of a successful business strategy. Building a customer-centric culture ensures that every employee is committed to delivering the best possible service. Utilizing customer feedback helps in continuously improving the service offerings. Community involvement strengthens the bond between the business and its customers, creating a sense of loyalty and trust. Effective reputation management safeguards and enhances the brand's image in the public eye. Together, these elements create a holistic approach that not only attracts customers but turns them into advocates for the brand.

Fostering a customer-centric culture requires a shift in mindset at every level of the organization. This shift is about seeing every customer interaction as an opportunity to deliver value and exceed expectations. Training should focus on soft skills like empathy, communication, and problem-solving, which are key to understanding and meeting customer needs. Leaders should set an example by engaging with customers personally and showing a genuine interest in their feedback.

Actively utilizing customer feedback is about creating a loop where customer input directly influences service improvements. This feedback should be systematically collected, analyzed, and acted upon. It's not just about resolving complaints but understanding the underlying issues and making necessary changes in the business process or service delivery. Celebrating feedback, even when it's critical, fosters a culture of transparency and continuous improvement.

Community involvement should go beyond mere tokenism or marketing tactics. It's about finding meaningful ways to contribute to the community that align with the business's core values and expertise. This could range from sponsoring local sports teams to participating in community service projects or hosting events that benefit local causes.

Such involvement demonstrates that the business is invested in the community's wellbeing, which can create deep, lasting ties with local customers.

Managing a brand's reputation in the digital era requires vigilance and responsiveness. Businesses should actively monitor their online presence, address negative feedback promptly, and engage in conversations with customers. A proactive approach to reputation management also involves sharing positive stories and customer experiences, showcasing the brand's commitment to excellence in service.

Incorporating these strategies into the business model can lead to a significant competitive advantage. A business known for its exceptional customer service, active community involvement, and positive online presence is likely to attract more customers, foster greater loyalty, and enjoy a stronger reputation. In the long run, these factors contribute to sustained business growth and success.

Growth and Expansion Opportunities

In the bustling world of business, growth and expansion are not just indicators of success, but they are also vital for the long-term sustainability of any venture. For business owners, identifying and capitalizing on expansion opportunities is akin to a gardener nurturing and growing their garden, where each new branch is a testament to their hard work and foresight. This journey of expansion, however, requires careful planning, adequate financing, and a keen eye for risk assessment.

The first step in the journey of growth is identifying potential areas for expansion. This could mean exploring new markets that are ripe for your services or products, opening additional locations in underserved areas, or diversifying the range of services or products offered. The key here is thorough market research. Understanding the needs and preferences of customers in new markets, or identifying gaps in your current market, can reveal lucrative opportunities for expansion.

* * *

Picture a local coffee shop that's become a neighborhood favorite. The owner notices that customers often ask about coffee beans for home brewing. Sensing an opportunity, they consider expanding the business to include selling coffee beans and brewing equipment. This kind of service diversification not only meets customer needs but also opens up new revenue streams. Similarly, expanding into new geographical locations can be a game-changer, especially if these areas have a demand for your products or services but lack adequate supply.

Strategic Planning for Expansion

Once potential areas for growth are identified, the next crucial step is strategic planning. This involves a comprehensive analysis of market trends, competitive landscape, and consumer behavior. It's essential to align your expansion plan with the overall vision and growth policies of your franchisor, if applicable. This strategic plan should detail the operational, marketing, and financial aspects of the expansion.

Imagine our coffee shop owner again. They would need to plan how to source coffee beans, decide whether to roast them in-house or partner with suppliers, and determine how to market this new line of products. They would also need to consider how this expansion aligns with their brand image and the customer experience they want to deliver.

Financing is the fuel for your expansion engine. When looking at funding options, there are several paths to consider. Traditional bank loans are a common choice, but they come with their set of requirements and conditions. Some franchisors offer financing options, which can be a convenient route since they already understand the business model and potential. Another avenue is forming partnerships with investors who are willing to provide capital in exchange for a stake in the business.

Each funding option has its pros and cons, and the right choice depends on your business's financial health, the terms of the financing, and your comfort with sharing control if you opt for investor partnerships. It's like choosing between a manual, an automatic, or an electric vehicle, each offering a different driving experience and set of responsibilities.

Risk Assessment

With great expansion comes great responsibility, including the need to assess and mitigate risks. Expansion is inherently risky – there are chances of overextending financially, misjudging the market, or facing operational challenges. A thorough risk assessment involves evaluating these potential hurdles and developing strategies to address them. This means looking at financial risks, such as the burden of loans, market risks like changing consumer preferences or economic downturns, and operational risks associated with scaling up the business.

Our coffee shop owner, for instance, needs to consider risks such as the potential of the new product line cannibalizing existing sales, or the challenges in maintaining quality and service standards with an expanded operation. They might mitigate these risks by conducting a pilot launch of the new product line in a limited area or ensuring that the expansion does not compromise the core values and qualities that made the coffee shop popular in the first place.

Risk assessment also involves contingency planning – having a backup plan if things don't go as expected. This could mean setting aside a financial cushion to handle unexpected expenses or challenges, or having a flexible business model that can adapt to changing market conditions.

Expanding a business is an exciting, albeit challenging, endeavor. It's like embarking on a voyage where the right tools, a well-thought-out map, and preparedness for unforeseen circumstances determine the success of the journey. Identifying expansion potential is about understanding where new opportunities lie and whether they align with your business goals and capabilities. Strategic planning is about charting a course for reaching these new destinations effectively and efficiently. Financing the growth is about finding the right partners and means to fuel your journey. And risk assessment is about being prepared for storms and choppy waters, ensuring that your business remains resilient and adaptable.

In essence, growth and expansion are not just about reaching new heights but doing so sustainably and responsibly. It's about nurturing the garden of your business, planting new seeds thoughtfully, and ensuring they have the right conditions to flourish. With careful planning, judicious financing, and strategic risk management, the opportunities for growth and expansion can be boundless, leading to a thriving, robust business that stands the test of time and change.

Dealing With Franchise Challenges and Setbacks

In the journey of running a franchise, encountering challenges and setbacks is as inevitable as the changing seasons. These hurdles, ranging from market fluctuations and competitive pressures to operational challenges, are part and parcel of the business landscape. However, the true mettle of a franchisee is tested not by the presence of these challenges but by their ability to navigate through them effectively.

Franchisees often face a myriad of obstacles that can test their resilience and business acumen. Market fluctuations, for instance, can dramatically alter consumer behavior and spending, impacting sales and profitability. Competitive pressures, especially in saturated markets, pose a significant challenge as franchises strive to maintain a unique value proposition and customer loyalty. Operational hurdles, such as supply chain disruptions, staffing issues, or regulatory changes, can also derail the smooth functioning of a franchise.

Consider a franchise in the food industry; a sudden shift in market trends towards healthier eating can significantly impact a business that primarily offers fast food. Similarly, an influx of similar businesses in the vicinity can intensify competition, requiring innovative strategies to attract and retain customers.

* * *

Crisis Management Strategies

When faced with unforeseen crises like economic downturns or operational disruptions, effective crisis management strategies become crucial. The first step in managing any crisis is to assess the situation comprehensively and respond promptly. This involves understanding the scope of the crisis, its potential impact on the business, and the resources available to address it.

Communication is key during a crisis. Keeping employees, customers, and franchisors informed and engaged can help manage expectations and reduce panic. Flexibility in operations and the ability to pivot business strategies quickly can also be a significant advantage. For instance, during the COVID-19 pandemic, many restaurants quickly shifted to online ordering and delivery models to adapt to the changing environment.

Every challenge or setback carries with it a valuable lesson. Successful franchisees understand that these difficulties are not just obstacles but opportunities for learning and growth. Analyzing what went wrong, what could have been done differently, and how to prevent similar issues in the future is essential. This approach not only helps in improving business practices but also builds resilience.

For example, if a marketing campaign fails to yield expected results, it provides an opportunity to delve into customer insights and market trends, potentially leading to more effective future campaigns. Similarly, if a new product launch doesn't perform as anticipated, it can offer insights into customer preferences and product positioning strategies.

Seeking Support

One of the significant advantages of being part of a franchise is access to a network of support. Franchisors typically have a wealth of resources and experience that franchisees can tap into when facing difficulties. These resources might include training programs, marketing tools, operational guidelines, or even financial assistance.

Reaching out to the franchisor for guidance can provide valuable insights and strategies for overcoming specific challenges.

Additionally, engaging with other franchisees and professional networks can offer practical advice and moral support. Networking with peers can provide a platform to share experiences, learn from each other's mistakes and successes, and gain different perspectives on tackling common challenges.

Professional associations specific to the industry or franchising in general can also be a valuable resource. These organizations often provide educational materials, host workshops and seminars, and offer networking opportunities that can be instrumental in navigating through tough times.

Dealing with challenges and setbacks is an integral part of running a franchise. The key to successfully navigating these obstacles lies in understanding the common challenges, developing effective crisis management strategies, learning from setbacks, and utilizing available support systems. By adopting a proactive and resilient approach, franchisees can turn these challenges into catalysts for growth and improvement. This journey of overcoming difficulties not only strengthens the business but also enriches the franchisee's skills and experience, laying a solid foundation for long-term success and sustainability.

Conclusion

As we reach the conclusion of this chapter, it's essential to reflect on the critical management aspects that are integral to running a successful franchise. The journey of a franchisee is one of continuous evolution and adaptation, where learning and strategic thinking are paramount.

Successful franchise management encompasses several key areas:

- **Financial Management and Budgeting:** Mastery in financial planning, budgeting, and efficient allocation of resources is foundational. This includes understanding revenue streams, controlling expenses, and making informed financial decisions.

- **Operational Strategies:** Streamlined operations, compliance with franchisor standards, leveraging technology, and effective supply chain management are crucial for operational efficiency and service excellence.

- **Customer Service and Community Engagement:** Building a customer-centric culture, actively using customer feedback, engaging with the community, and managing the franchise's reputation online and offline are essential for long-term success.

- **Growth and Expansion:** Identifying and strategically planning for expansion opportunities, understanding financing options, and conducting thorough risk assessments are necessary for sustainable growth.

- **Dealing with Challenges:** Recognizing common franchise challenges, developing crisis management strategies, learning from setbacks, and seeking support from franchisors and professional networks are vital for resilience.

Franchisees are encouraged to continually evolve their management practices in alignment with business growth and market changes. This involves staying informed about industry trends, being open to new ideas, and adapting strategies as necessary. The business landscape is dynamic, and so should be the approach to managing a franchise.

The Importance of Adaptability, Learning, and Strategic Thinking

Adaptability, continuous learning, and strategic thinking are the hallmarks of successful franchise management. The ability to adapt to changing market conditions, learn from experiences (both successes and failures), and think strategically about the future is what differentiates thriving franchises from the rest.

* * *

Additional Resources

For franchisees looking to deepen their understanding and enhance their skills, numerous resources are available:

Franchise Associations and Networking Groups: These platforms offer valuable insights, networking opportunities, and resources tailored to the franchising industry.

Business Management Courses: Many online and offline courses are available that focus on specific aspects of franchise management, such as financial planning, marketing, and operations.

Industry Conferences and Seminars: Attending these events can provide insights into the latest trends and strategies in the franchising world.

Books and Publications: There are many books and industry publications that offer deep dives into the nuances of managing a successful franchise.

Mentorship and Coaching: Seeking mentors or coaches who have experience in franchising can offer personalized guidance and support, helping you navigate through unique challenges and opportunities.

In conclusion, managing a franchise successfully requires a blend of robust financial acumen, operational efficiency, exceptional customer service, strategic growth planning, and the resilience to overcome challenges. By embracing adaptability, committing to continuous learning, and employing strategic thinking, franchisees can navigate the complexities of the business landscape and steer their ventures towards sustained success. The journey of a franchisee is one of constant evolution, where every challenge is an opportunity for growth and every success a stepping stone to greater achievements. With the right resources and a steadfast commitment to excellence, the potential for achievement in the world of franchising is limitless. Remember, the most successful franchisees are those who not only excel in day-to-day management but also have the foresight to anticipate changes, adapt strategies, and continually strive for improvement. This proactive approach, coupled with a deep understanding of the intricacies of franchise management, sets the stage for enduring success and fulfillment in the exciting and ever-evolving world of franchising.

CHAPTER SEVEN

NETWORKING AND BUILDING RELATIONSHIPS

In the dynamic landscape of franchising, networking is the strategic process of building and nurturing professional relationships that are mutually beneficial. It involves connecting with fellow franchisees, industry experts, suppliers, and local communities to exchange information, share experiences, and foster collaboration. The significance of networking in the franchise industry cannot be overstated. It serves as a vital tool for gaining insights into market trends, overcoming operational challenges, and discovering new opportunities for growth. Networking in franchising transcends mere acquaintance-making; it's about forging connections that can lead to real-time business advantages, learning opportunities, and support systems that are crucial for navigating the complexities of the franchise business model.

This chapter aims to delve deep into the world of networking within the franchise sector, highlighting its indispensable role in the growth and sustainability of a franchise business. We will explore various facets of networking, starting from engaging with fellow franchisees and industry experts, which can provide a wealth of knowledge and experience. The chapter will then guide you through leveraging online resources and forums, a modern necessity for broadening your networking scope and staying updated with industry trends. Building and maintaining relationships with suppliers will be discussed as a cornerstone for operational success. Additionally, we will emphasize the importance of embedding oneself within the local community, which can be a bedrock of support and customer loyalty.

* * *

By the end of this chapter, the objective is to equip franchisees with comprehensive knowledge and practical strategies for effective networking. We aim to underscore the importance of adaptability, continuous learning, and strategic relationship-building in the realm of franchising. Whether you are new to the franchise world or a seasoned professional, this chapter promises to offer valuable insights into making networking a powerful tool for your business's success.

The Importance of Networking in Franchising

In the world of franchising, networking stands as a beacon of opportunity and growth. It's not just about exchanging business cards or attending social events; it's a strategic process that opens doors to new possibilities, collaborations, and insights. Networking can lead to increased referrals, access to valuable resources, and new business opportunities. It's a powerful tool that helps franchisees to connect not just within their own franchise system, but also across the broader business community.

For instance, consider a franchisee who regularly attends industry meetups. Here, they might encounter a supplier offering innovative products at a competitive rate, or they might learn about an emerging market trend from a fellow attendee. These interactions can lead to cost savings, improved product offerings, or even expansion into new markets. In essence, networking fosters a symbiotic ecosystem where franchisees can support and be supported, leading to mutual growth and success.

Networking is a conduit for the flow of ideas and solutions. Franchisees, particularly those new to the industry, often face a steep learning curve. By engaging with experienced peers and industry veterans, they can gain insights into effective business strategies, avoid common pitfalls, and find innovative solutions to challenges.

Imagine a scenario where a franchisee is struggling with a specific operational issue. Through networking, they might discover that another franchisee encountered a similar problem and found an efficient solution. This exchange of knowledge not only solves immediate problems but also contributes to a richer, more informed approach to business management. Networking events, forums, and even informal gatherings can become platforms for brainstorming, advice, and support, proving invaluable in navigating the complex waters of franchising.

In the fast-paced business world, staying updated with market trends and consumer preferences is crucial. Networking places franchisees at the forefront of industry developments. Through regular interaction with peers, experts, and suppliers, franchisees can stay attuned to the latest market shifts, consumer behaviors, and technological advancements.

Consider the impact of digital transformation across industries. A franchisee, through their network, might learn about the latest digital marketing strategies or e-commerce platforms that could significantly boost their business's online presence and sales. Networking events often feature guest speakers or panels discussing such trends, providing franchisees with a front-row seat to the evolving business landscape.

Moreover, understanding market trends through networking can be pivotal in making strategic business decisions. For example, a franchisee in the food industry might learn about the growing demand for plant-based options through discussions at a networking event. This insight could lead them to adapt their menu accordingly, capitalizing on a growing market segment and staying ahead of competitors.

Networking also opens the door to collaborative opportunities that might not have been apparent within the confines of one's own business. This could range from joint marketing efforts with non-competing businesses to exploring new distribution channels or co-branding opportunities. Such collaborations can expand a franchisee's reach and impact in ways that single-handed efforts might not achieve.

We're on the verge of beating it to death, but the compounding benefits of networking cannot be overstated. It's a vital tool for business growth, knowledge sharing, problem-solving, and staying abreast of market trends. By investing time and effort in building and nurturing a diverse professional network, franchisees can unlock new opportunities, gain valuable insights, and propel their business to greater heights. Networking isn't just about expanding one's business contacts; it's about actively participating in a community of like-minded professionals, all striving for success in the challenging yet rewarding world of franchising. With the right approach, networking can become one of the most powerful tools in a franchisee's arsenal for achieving sustained growth and success.

Networking With Other Franchisees and Industry Experts

Engaging with fellow franchisees and industry experts is a fundamental aspect of achieving success in the franchise business world. This chapter explores the numerous benefits and opportunities that stem from such interactions, highlighting the significance of collaboration, learning, and mutual growth within the franchise industry.

Benefits of Connecting with Fellow Franchisees

The franchise model thrives on the sharing of best practices and experiences. By connecting with fellow franchisees, individuals gain access to practical knowledge and real-life experiences. This sharing isn't just about successes; it's also learning from others' mistakes, helping to save time, resources, and avoid common pitfalls. For instance, a franchisee in the food industry might share insights on efficient inventory management or customer service techniques that have significantly improved their operations. These shared experiences, grounded in practice rather than theory, often lead to more efficient and profitable operations across the franchise network.

Such interactions foster a sense of community, especially beneficial for new franchisees navigating the initial challenges of their business. This camaraderie creates a support system where franchisees feel more secure and supported in their entrepreneurial journey. Additionally, these interactions often lead to collaborative opportunities and joint ventures, like marketing initiatives or bulk purchasing, reducing costs and increasing bargaining power with suppliers. For example, retail franchisees might collaborate on regional advertising campaigns, sharing costs for greater market reach.

Learning from Industry Experts

Engaging with industry experts provides franchisees with access to specialized knowledge, mentorship, and guidance. These seasoned professionals can offer insights not typically available through standard training programs or operational manuals, helping franchisees navigate complex issues and develop a strategic business outlook. For instance, an expert in the fast-food sector might provide advice on optimizing supply chain logistics, a common challenge for many franchisees.

Participation in workshops and seminars led by these experts offers immersive learning experiences, where franchisees can update their skills, learn about emerging trends, and adapt to market demands. These events are also excellent networking opportunities, fostering relationships that can lead to future collaborations or mentorships.

In conclusion, engaging with other franchisees and industry experts is crucial for the success and sustainability of a franchise operation. It provides a platform for shared knowledge, practical advice, and innovative ideas. Collaborative efforts stemming from these interactions not only lead to cost savings but also foster a culture of innovation and support. Mentorship from industry experts complements franchisees' experiences, offering advice on daily operations and long-term strategic planning. Additionally, workshops and seminars ensure franchisees remain updated with industry trends and best practices, vital in an ever-evolving market. This collective knowledge and unity within the franchise network significantly enhance individual business success and the overall strength of the franchise system.

* * *

Leveraging Online Resources and Forums

In today's digital era, the strategic use of online resources and forums has become crucial in the growth and management of a franchise business. This chapter aims to delve into the effective utilization of these digital platforms, providing a comprehensive guide for franchisees.

The journey into the digital world begins with identifying the right online platforms and forums pertinent to your franchise business. It's essential to pinpoint where your target audience, fellow franchisees, and industry experts congregate. The digital landscape offers a plethora of platforms, from broad social networks like LinkedIn and Facebook to niche forums focused on specific industries or business topics.

For franchisees, it's beneficial to engage in industry-specific forums to connect with peers, and broader entrepreneurial sites for insights into business management and growth. Platforms like Reddit and Quora are invaluable for gaining diverse perspectives and practical solutions to unique challenges. Choosing the right platform depends on the nature of your franchise, the target market, and where relevant discussions are most active. Evaluating the credibility of these platforms ensures the reliability of the information accessed and shared.

Best Practices for Engaging in Online Communities

Having identified relevant platforms, effective engagement within these communities is paramount. Key practices include being an active participant, not just by posting queries or insights but by responding to others, sharing experiences, and offering advice. This active engagement helps build a reputation as a knowledgeable and supportive community member.

Providing value in interactions, whether through insightful articles, practical solutions, or new perspectives, is crucial. Professionalism in online interactions reflects on both you and your franchise brand, so it's important to maintain a respectful tone, even in disagreements.

Authentic networking builds more meaningful relationships than merely adding contacts. Engage in genuine conversations, show interest in others' posts, and offer assistance where possible. These forums are also valuable learning resources, offering insights on industry trends and new strategies. Keeping an open mind and willingness to learn from others is essential.

Respecting privacy and confidentiality is critical. Avoid sharing sensitive information about your franchise or discussing topics that could violate agreements or harm your brand.

Utilizing Online Networks for Market Research and Brand Visibility

Online platforms serve as powerful tools for market research and enhancing brand visibility. They provide insights into customer opinions, industry trends, and competitor strategies. Observing discussions and questions in these forums can yield valuable data on customer needs and preferences, which can inform marketing strategies, product development, and customer service approaches.

Active participation in relevant online discussions increases the visibility of your franchise brand. Sharing successes and learnings, participating in conversations, and positioning yourself as a thought leader can elevate both your personal and franchise brand.

Social media platforms are effective for franchise promotion, offering avenues for engaging content sharing, targeted advertising, and interactive communication with followers, thereby expanding your brand's reach and attracting potential customers.

Engaging with influencers or forming partnerships within your online network can also enhance your franchise's credibility and exposure. These collaborations can open doors to new audiences and lend additional credibility to your brand.

* * *

In summary, harnessing online resources and forums effectively can bring manifold benefits to a franchise business. These digital platforms serve as invaluable tools for networking, learning, market research, and increasing brand visibility. Franchisees can gather diverse insights, stay abreast of industry trends, and engage in meaningful dialogue with peers and experts. Actively participating in these online communities not only enhances personal and brand reputation but also contributes to the strategic growth and visibility of the franchise. It's crucial, however, to navigate these digital arenas with professionalism, authenticity, and a strategic approach to fully reap their benefits. The digital landscape offers a rich array of opportunities for franchisees willing to explore, engage, and innovate in the evolving world of franchising.

The Importance of Strong Supplier Relationships in Franchising

At the heart of franchising lies a dependency on consistent quality and service, elements heavily influenced by suppliers. A strong supplier relationship guarantees a regular supply of high-quality products or services, crucial for upholding the brand's reputation and ensuring customer satisfaction. These relationships form the operational backbone of a franchise, contributing to its efficiency and effectiveness.

Beyond providing timely and quality supplies, robust supplier relationships can yield preferential pricing, favorable payment terms, and early access to new products or innovations. Such advantages significantly bolster a franchise's competitive market stance. In challenging times, like supply chain disruptions, these strong relationships can be the difference between a minor hiccup and a major operational crisis. Suppliers with a positive, long-standing relationship with a franchise are more likely to extend extra support in difficult times.

Strategies for Effective Supplier Management and

Negotiation

Effective supplier management and negotiation start with a deep understanding of the supplier's business and needs, fostering a mutually beneficial relationship. Essential strategies include:

Conducting Thorough Research: Before negotiations, gathering extensive information about the supplier can provide leverage. Understanding their market position, strengths, and weaknesses is key.

Building Mutual Trust: Trust is foundational in business relationships. Maintaining transparency, honoring commitments, and effective communication build a solid trust foundation.

Negotiating Fairly: It's vital to negotiate terms favorable to your franchise but also ensure the deal is fair and sustainable for the supplier. Unreasonable demands can strain the relationship.

Leveraging Collective Buying Power: Utilize the collective power of the franchise network to negotiate better deals. Suppliers often offer more favorable terms for larger, consolidated orders.

Regular Reviews and Feedback: Consistent performance review and constructive feedback help maintain quality and address issues proactively.

Fostering Long-Term Relationships: Prioritize long-term partnerships over short-term gains. Long-term relationships often lead to better service, loyalty, and terms over time.

Long-Term Benefits of Reliable Supplier Partnerships

Reliable supplier partnerships are a cornerstone of success in franchising, offering a multitude of long-term benefits that extend far beyond the immediate transactional interactions. These partnerships ensure consistency in the quality and supply of products or services, which is crucial for maintaining customer satisfaction and the uniformity of the brand. Such consistency is foundational for building and sustaining customer loyalty.

Moreover, long-standing relationships with suppliers often lead to cost efficiency. These enduring partnerships can result in more favorable pricing and terms, directly improving the profitability of a franchise. This aspect of cost efficiency is particularly crucial in a competitive market, where maintaining a balance between quality and affordability is key to attracting and retaining customers.

Access to innovations and improvements is another significant benefit of strong supplier relationships. Suppliers who view a franchise as a valued partner are more inclined to share new products or innovations. This access can provide a franchise with a competitive edge, allowing it to offer the latest products or services and quickly adapt to changing market demands.

In terms of risk mitigation, robust supplier relationships act as a buffer during times of market volatility or supply chain disruptions. Suppliers with a vested interest in a franchise's success are more likely to extend support during challenging times, ensuring operational continuity and minimizing disruptions.

These partnerships also enhance a franchise's reputation and open doors to networking opportunities. Being associated with reputable and reliable suppliers can bolster a franchise's image in the market. Furthermore, good supplier relations often lead to introductions to other potential partners, expanding the franchise's network and its possibilities for growth.

Collaborative problem-solving is another hallmark of strong supplier relationships. Suppliers who have a long-term, positive partnership with a franchise are more likely to work together to find solutions to various challenges, be it adjusting delivery schedules, exploring alternative products, or modifying order quantities.

Lastly, a valuable feedback loop for operational improvement is established through these partnerships. Suppliers, with their unique perspective on the market and operations, can offer insightful feedback that can be instrumental in improving various aspects of a franchise's operation, from logistics to inventory management. This two-way feedback loop is invaluable for continuous improvement and innovation, driving the franchise towards greater efficiency and success.

In essence, cultivating reliable supplier partnerships is not just a strategic necessity but a significant contributor to the overall growth and sustainability of a franchise. These relationships provide stability, support, and opportunities for advancement, playing a crucial role in the franchise's journey towards long-term success and resilience. By prioritizing and nurturing these relationships, franchisees unlock a wealth of opportunities that drive their businesses forward in an effective, efficient, and sustainable manner.

Approaching supplier relationships with a strategy that aligns with long-term business goals means focusing on more than just securing favorable terms; it involves cultivating mutual respect, collaboration, and shared growth objectives. By doing so, franchises can transform their supplier relationships into one of their most significant assets, laying a stable foundation for a thriving business.

As franchises navigate an increasingly complex and competitive business landscape, the significance of robust supplier relationships becomes even more pronounced. These partnerships are more than transactional interactions; they are strategic alliances that can propel a franchise toward long-term success and resilience. Prioritizing and nurturing these relationships, franchisees can unlock a wealth of opportunities, driving their businesses forward in an effective and sustainable manner.

Connecting with the Local Community

In the realm of franchising, forging a bond with the local community is not just beneficial; it's a cornerstone of business growth and sustainability. Community engagement goes beyond mere presence; it's an active, ongoing process of building relationships, understanding local needs, and contributing meaningfully to the community's fabric.

A franchise's success is deeply intertwined with its reputation and relationships within its local community. When a franchise becomes a recognized and respected entity, not just as a business but as a contributing member of the community, it paves the way for enduring success. This connection leads to increased trust and loyalty among local customers, which are vital in today's competitive market.

One effective strategy is participating in and sponsoring local events. This involvement shows that the franchise is invested in the community's well-being and is interested in more than just business transactions. Whether it's sponsoring a local sports team, participating in charity events, or organizing community activities, these actions help in building a positive brand image and foster goodwill.

Moreover, establishing local collaborations and partnerships can be tremendously beneficial. By partnering with other local businesses or community organizations, a franchise can integrate itself more deeply into the local fabric. These collaborations can range from joint marketing campaigns with other businesses to supporting local causes. Such partnerships not only increase the franchise's visibility but also create a network of mutual support, essential for long-term survival and growth.

Measuring the impact of these community engagement efforts is crucial. This can be done through customer feedback, increases in foot traffic, or community response to events and initiatives. For example, a noticeable increase in sales following a community event or a rise in social media engagement from the local area can be indicators of successful community integration.

Best Practices in Networking and Relationship Building

Effective networking and communication are key to building these relationships. Tips for successful networking include being genuine in interactions, actively listening, and providing value in every exchange. It's about creating meaningful connections rather than just exchanging business cards.

Balancing online and offline networking strategies is also vital. While social media and online platforms offer vast networking opportunities, they should complement, not replace, face-to-face interactions. Personal meetings, attending local business events, and participating in community gatherings are irreplaceable for building deep and lasting relationships.

Continuously nurturing and expanding your network is a continuous process. It involves regular follow-ups, staying in touch with contacts, and being proactive in seeking new connections. It's about creating a network that's not just wide but also deep, with relationships based on mutual respect and support.

In conclusion, connecting with the local community and effective networking are not just strategies; they are essential practices for any franchise's growth and sustainability. By embedding themselves within the local community and building a strong network, franchises can create a robust foundation for long-term success. This approach leads to a franchise that is not only a business entity but a valued and integral part of the community it serves.

Overcoming Challenges in Networking

Networking, an indispensable tool in the business world, often presents a multitude of challenges. From the hesitant novice to the seasoned professional, everyone faces hurdles in building and maintaining effective networks. This chapter explores the common obstacles encountered in networking, offers strategies to enhance networking skills and confidence, and discusses adapting networking approaches in changing business environments.

One of the primary challenges in networking is the discomfort or apprehension associated with initiating conversations with strangers. Many individuals struggle with this aspect, especially in formal networking environments. This discomfort can stem from a fear of rejection, a lack of confidence, or simply not knowing what to say.

Another common hurdle is maintaining and nurturing connections. After initial contacts are made, it can be challenging to keep these relationships alive and beneficial. Busy schedules, forgetfulness, or uncertainty about how to add value to these connections can lead to neglected networks that gradually lose their potential.

A more modern challenge in networking is the overwhelming nature of online platforms. While these platforms offer incredible opportunities for connection, they can also lead to information overload and a lack of genuine, meaningful interactions. Differentiating oneself in a sea of digital profiles and maintaining authentic connections can be daunting tasks.

Enhancing networking skills begins with overcoming the fear of initiating conversations. One effective method is to prepare conversation starters or questions in advance. This preparation can alleviate the anxiety associated with starting a conversation. Practicing active listening is also crucial. Showing genuine interest in others and their perspectives not only makes conversations easier but also helps build more meaningful connections.

Building confidence in networking often involves stepping out of one's comfort zone. Attending various types of networking events, both within and outside one's industry, can provide diverse experiences that bolster confidence. Setting small, achievable goals for each networking event, such as initiating conversations with a certain number of people, can also be a confidence-building exercise.

Another key strategy is to focus on quality over quantity. Rather than trying to connect with everyone, it's more beneficial to cultivate deeper relationships with fewer people. These quality connections are more likely to be mutually beneficial and enduring.

Adapting Networking Approaches in Changing Business Environments

In today's rapidly evolving business landscape, adapting networking strategies is crucial. One significant shift is the increasing reliance on digital platforms for networking. While these platforms offer convenience and a broader reach, they also require a different set of skills. To stand out in the digital realm, it is essential to have a clear, compelling online presence. This includes a professional profile on platforms like LinkedIn, an active engagement in industry-related groups, and sharing of relevant content that showcases expertise and interests.

Another aspect of adaptation is recognizing and embracing the diversity in networking environments. Today's global business landscape means encountering a wide array of cultures, professions, and perspectives. Being culturally sensitive and open to different viewpoints not only enriches the networking experience but also broadens one's understanding and acceptance, which are critical in today's interconnected world.

In addition, the rise of niche networking events and platforms offers opportunities to connect with like-minded individuals or those in specific industries. Attending these targeted events or joining specialized online communities can lead to more meaningful and focused networking opportunities.

The ability to network virtually has also become essential. With the increase in remote working and virtual meetings, being able to effectively connect and communicate through a screen is as important as face-to-face interactions. This includes mastering the etiquette of virtual meetings, being comfortable with video conferencing tools, and finding creative ways to engage and follow up digitally.

Moreover, the concept of networking has expanded beyond just business relationships. There is a growing emphasis on building networks that also offer personal growth, learning opportunities, and support. This holistic approach to networking recognizes that personal and professional development are intertwined, and that relationships built on mutual growth and support can be particularly powerful.

In the context of ever-changing business environments, continuous learning and adaptation in networking strategies are vital. Staying informed about trends, being open to new technologies and platforms, and being willing to experiment with different approaches are key to successful networking in a dynamic world.

In conclusion, overcoming challenges in networking requires a combination of personal development, skill enhancement, and adaptability to changing environments. By addressing common hurdles, enhancing networking skills and confidence, and adapting to the evolving business landscape, individuals can build and maintain networks that not only contribute to their professional success but also enrich their personal experiences. Networking is not just a business tool; it's a continuous journey of building relationships, learning, and growing in an interconnected world.

Conclusion

As we conclude this guide on the importance of networking and relationship building in franchising, we reflect on the essential role these practices play in fostering business growth and sustainability. Key takeaways include the invaluable benefits of engaging with the local community, navigating and overcoming networking challenges, and adapting to the ever-evolving business landscape. Effective networking transcends mere contact expansion; it's about cultivating meaningful and mutually beneficial relationships. Strategies like participating in community events, collaborating with local businesses, and making the most of both online and offline platforms have been emphasized as critical to developing a robust network.

In the world of franchising, the ongoing importance of networking and relationship building can't be overstated. These practices are central to gaining insights, sharing experiences, and maintaining a competitive edge. Networking is instrumental in understanding customer needs, keeping abreast of industry trends, and forging valuable partnerships that lead to new opportunities for growth. The strength of a franchise is often a reflection of the robustness of its network and its ability to foster dynamic, supportive relationships within the community and industry.

Franchisees are encouraged to adopt a proactive approach to networking and community engagement. This involves active participation in relevant events, maintaining a strong presence on professional platforms, and continually seeking collaborative opportunities. Such engagement not only bolsters the franchise's reputation but also deepens its connection with customers. By integrating networking and relationship building into their growth strategy, franchisees ensure these activities are continuous and integral to their business development.

For those seeking to expand their knowledge and skills in this area, a wealth of resources is available. Recommended readings such as Keith Ferrazzi's **"Never Eat Alone"** provide valuable insights into cultivating professional relationships. Online platforms like Harvard Business Review and Entrepreneur offer a treasure trove of articles and tips on effective networking and business development strategies. Additionally, platforms like LinkedIn Learning present a range of courses and webinars dedicated to enhancing networking skills.

Joining networking groups and professional associations can also be invaluable. For franchise owners, being part of organizations such as the International Franchise Association (IFA) can provide opportunities to connect with industry peers, experts, and potential partners. Local business chambers and industry-specific associations offer further networking prospects and resources tailored to specific business needs.

Furthermore, attending networking events and conferences is a powerful way to build relationships, stay informed about industry trends, and gain new insights. Events like the Franchise Times Finance & Growth Conference or the Multi-Unit Franchising Conference are not only ideal for networking but also offer educational workshops and sessions. Regularly checking industry websites and newsletters for updates on such events can keep franchisees informed and prepared to take advantage of these opportunities.

In summary, the journey of networking and relationship building in the world of franchising is a continuous and evolving process. It demands a proactive and committed approach, a readiness to learn and adapt, and a focus on forging genuine, enduring relationships. By embracing these principles and utilizing the resources at their disposal, franchise owners can open new doors for growth and success. They can establish their businesses as integral, respected members of their communities and industries, laying a solid foundation for long-term achievement and recognition in the franchising sector.

CHAPTER EIGHT

THE FRANCHISOR-FRANCHISEE RELATIONSHIP

The relationship between a franchisor and a franchisee is a fundamental element of the franchise business model. This dynamic is characterized by a unique blend of interdependence and autonomy. The franchisor, who owns the overarching brand and business system, grants the franchisee the right to operate a business under this brand and system. In return, the franchisee pays certain fees and agrees to adhere to the franchisor's established practices and guidelines.

This relationship is much more than a simple buyer-seller interaction. It's a complex partnership where both parties work towards a common goal: the success and growth of the brand. The franchisor provides the franchisee with a proven business model, brand recognition, and ongoing support. This support can include training, marketing strategies, product development, and operational guidelines. The franchisee, in turn, brings local market knowledge, entrepreneurial spirit, and a commitment to maintaining the brand's standards and reputation at the local level.

Importance of This Partnership in the Franchise Model

The significance of this partnership cannot be overstated in the context of the franchising model. It serves as the backbone of the franchising concept, where success is heavily reliant on the strength and quality of the relationship between franchisor and franchisee. A well-functioning franchisor-franchisee relationship can lead to numerous benefits, including:

Brand Consistency: The franchisor-franchisee partnership ensures that customers experience the same quality of service and products across different locations, reinforcing brand consistency and trust.

Scalability and Growth: Through this partnership, franchisors can expand their brand more rapidly and efficiently than they could by opening new locations themselves. Franchisees, leveraging the franchisor's brand and system, can establish successful businesses with a lower risk than starting from scratch.

Innovation and Adaptation: Franchisees often bring valuable on-the-ground insights that can drive innovation and adaptation within the franchise system. Their feedback can lead to improvements in operations, marketing strategies, and even product offerings.

Shared Success: The franchisor's success is directly tied to the success of its franchisees. As the franchisees' businesses grow, the franchisor benefits from increased brand recognition and financial returns. This interdependence creates a powerful incentive for franchisors to invest in the success of their franchisees.

In summary, the franchisor-franchisee relationship is a symbiotic one, with each party playing a crucial role in the overall success of the franchise. Understanding, nurturing, and optimizing this relationship is essential for the growth and sustainability of the franchise model.

Understanding the Dynamics of This Partnership

The dynamics of the franchisor-franchisee partnership form the cornerstone of the franchise business model. This section delves into the definitions and roles of both franchisors and franchisees, the legal and business framework that governs their relationship, and the mutual dependencies and benefits that underscore this unique business model.

Franchisors are entities or individuals who own the rights to a business brand and model. They are responsible for developing the overarching business strategy, brand standards, marketing initiatives, and operational procedures. The franchisor's role extends to providing training, support, and resources to franchisees to ensure the consistent delivery of the brand promise across all franchise units.

Franchisees, on the other hand, are independent business owners who purchase the right to operate a franchise under the franchisor's brand and system. They are responsible for the day-to-day management of their franchise unit, including hiring and training staff, managing operations, and adhering to the franchisor's established guidelines and standards. While they operate under the umbrella of the franchisor's brand, franchisees are responsible for the financial aspects of their individual franchise, including initial investment, operational costs, and profits.

The franchisor-franchisee relationship is governed by a complex legal and business framework, which is essential to ensure clarity, protect the interests of both parties, and maintain brand integrity.

The cornerstone of this framework is the Franchise Agreement, a legally binding contract that outlines the rights and responsibilities of both the franchisor and the franchisee. This agreement typically includes terms regarding the use of trademarks and proprietary information, duration of the franchise, renewal terms, financial arrangements (such as franchise fees, royalties, and advertising contributions), training and support, and grounds for termination.

Apart from the Franchise Agreement, various laws and regulations also govern this relationship. In the United States, for instance, the Federal Trade Commission requires franchisors to provide a Franchise Disclosure Document (FDD) to prospective franchisees. This document offers an extensive overview of the franchise opportunity, including a history of the franchisor, litigation history, financial statements, and a list of current and former franchisees.

Furthermore, many states have their franchise laws and regulations, often requiring additional disclosures or offering additional protections to franchisees. These legal frameworks ensure a level of transparency and fairness in the franchise relationship and protect both parties from potential disputes and misunderstandings.

Mutual Dependencies and Benefits

The franchisor-franchisee relationship is inherently symbiotic, with mutual dependencies and benefits.

Franchisors depend on franchisees to expand their brand and generate revenue. Franchisees, acting as local operators, provide market penetration and customer access that franchisors alone couldn't efficiently achieve. This expansion allows franchisors to grow their brand footprint rapidly while minimizing the capital investment and operational risks that come with opening new locations.

For franchisees, the primary benefit lies in the ability to start a business with an established brand and proven business model. This significantly reduces the risks typically associated with starting a new business. They gain access to an established customer base, brand recognition, comprehensive training programs, ongoing support, and the collective buying power of the franchising network.

Moreover, both parties benefit from shared knowledge and innovation. Franchisees, being on the front lines, can provide valuable feedback and market insights that can lead to improvements in products, services, and operational processes. This two-way flow of information and innovation enhances the brand's competitiveness and adaptability in the market.

In conclusion, the franchisor-franchisee relationship is a dynamic and complex partnership that demands clear understanding, mutual respect, and ongoing collaboration. Both parties play distinct but interdependent roles, governed by a comprehensive legal and business framework. This partnership not only facilitates the expansion and growth of the franchisor's brand but also provides franchisees with a robust platform to launch and grow their own businesses. The mutual dependencies and benefits that arise from this relationship create a powerful synergy, driving success for both franchisors and franchisees. It's a relationship built on the foundation of shared goals, with each party contributing unique strengths and resources towards a common objective – the growth and prosperity of the brand and its individual franchises.

By comprehensively understanding the dynamics of this partnership, franchisors and franchisees can effectively navigate the complexities of their relationship, leading to a more cohesive, productive, and profitable collaboration. This understanding is crucial not only for maintaining brand consistency and quality across different locations but also for fostering innovation, adapting to changing market conditions, and achieving long-term success in the competitive world of franchising.

Ultimately, the strength of the franchisor-franchisee relationship lies in its ability to balance the franchisor's need for control and standardization with the franchisee's entrepreneurial drive and local market expertise. When this balance is struck, it paves the way for a thriving, mutually beneficial partnership that is resilient, adaptable, and capable of weathering the challenges of the ever-evolving business landscape.

Communication and Collaboration Strategies

The success of the franchisor-franchisee relationship hinges significantly on the effectiveness of communication and the quality of collaboration between the two parties. This section explores the importance of open and effective communication, outlines best practices for fostering regular and constructive dialogue, delves into collaboration techniques for mutual success, and highlights the tools and technologies that facilitate these processes.

Effective communication is the lifeblood of any successful franchisor-franchisee relationship. It serves as a tool for sharing information, resolving conflicts, building trust, and fostering a shared vision. Open communication ensures that both parties are aligned in their goals, understand each other's expectations, and are aware of any issues or changes within the franchise system. It also enables franchisees to provide valuable feedback and insights to the franchisor, which can lead to improvements in operations, marketing strategies, and overall brand development.

Best Practices for Regular and Constructive Dialogue

Scheduled Regular Meetings: Regularly scheduled meetings, whether virtual or in-person, provide a structured opportunity for franchisors and franchisees to discuss ongoing operations, address concerns, and share successes. These meetings should be held consistently to maintain a steady flow of communication.

Clear and Transparent Communication: Clarity and transparency in communication help prevent misunderstandings and build trust. Franchisors should clearly communicate expectations, changes in policies, and any other pertinent information. Similarly, franchisees should be open about their challenges and successes.

Constructive Feedback Mechanisms: Implementing structured feedback mechanisms where franchisees can share their on-ground experiences and suggestions is crucial. This could be in the form of surveys, suggestion boxes, or regular feedback sessions.

Conflict Resolution Protocols: Having established protocols for conflict resolution ensures that when disagreements arise, they are handled constructively and effectively, preventing escalation and fostering a healthier business environment.

Collaboration Techniques for Mutual Success

Joint Problem-Solving: Encourage a culture where franchisors and franchisees work together to solve problems. This collaborative approach leverages the strengths and perspectives of both parties, leading to more effective solutions.

Shared Goals and Incentives: Establishing shared goals and aligning incentives ensures that both franchisors and franchisees work towards common objectives, creating a win-win situation. For instance, a franchisor might offer incentives for achieving certain performance metrics, aligning the franchisee's success with the brand's growth.

Collaborative Planning and Decision-Making: Involve franchisees in planning and decision-making processes, especially on matters that directly affect their operations. This inclusion not only provides franchisors with valuable insights but also ensures franchisees feel valued and invested in the brand's future.

Tools and Technologies Facilitating Communication

Franchise Management Software: Utilizing specialized software can streamline communication and operations. These platforms often include features for training, marketing, operations management, and performance tracking, ensuring that both franchisors and franchisees have access to the same information and resources.

Virtual Communication Platforms: Tools like Zoom, Microsoft Teams, or Skype facilitate regular virtual meetings, training sessions, and webinars, essential for maintaining consistent communication, especially in geographically dispersed franchise systems.

Collaborative Workspaces: Platforms like Slack or Asana enable real-time messaging, task management, and document sharing, fostering a collaborative environment where franchisors and franchisees can work together seamlessly.

CRM Systems: Customer Relationship Management (CRM) systems can be invaluable for sharing customer feedback, market data, and insights that help both franchisors and franchisees in making informed decisions.

Social Media and Community Forums: Leveraging social media and online forums can help build a community among franchisees, allowing them to share experiences, solutions, and best practices, further strengthening the network.

By implementing best practices for communication, adopting

collaborative strategies, and utilizing the right tools and technologies, franchisors and franchisees can establish a strong foundation for mutual success. Open and regular dialogue helps in aligning goals, understanding challenges, and celebrating successes, while collaboration fosters a sense of unity and shared purpose.

Through these strategies, the franchise system can become more than just a network of individual businesses; it can evolve into a cohesive, collaborative community, driving the brand forward. Effective communication and collaboration not only enhance operational efficiency and brand consistency but also contribute to a more innovative and adaptable franchise system.

Ultimately, the strength of the franchisor-franchisee relationship is measured not just by individual successes, but by the ability to work together towards common goals, adapt to changing market conditions, and continuously improve the franchise system for the benefit of all involved. This synergistic approach is what sets apart successful franchise models, ensuring long-term growth and sustainability in the competitive business landscape.

Managing Expectations and Resolving Conflicts

In the franchisor-franchisee dynamic, managing expectations and effectively resolving conflicts are pivotal to maintaining a healthy, productive relationship. This section explores setting realistic expectations, identifying common conflict sources, strategies for resolution, and the significance of ongoing support and training.

Realistic expectations form the bedrock of a healthy franchisor-franchisee relationship. For franchisors, this means being transparent about the support they can offer and the performance they expect. They must provide clear, detailed information about the business model, potential earnings, market challenges, and the level of autonomy the franchisee will have. It's crucial to avoid overpromising on business outcomes or underestimating the challenges.

Franchisees, in turn, should have realistic expectations about what it takes to make the franchise successful. This includes understanding the level of hard work, compliance to franchisor standards, financial commitment, and the time frame required to see a return on investment. Both parties must enter the relationship with a clear understanding of their roles, responsibilities, and the realities of the business landscape they are entering.

Conflicts in the franchisor-franchisee relationship often stem from misaligned expectations, communication breakdowns, or operational disagreements. One common source of conflict is financial performance and expectations. Franchisees might struggle to meet the sales targets or find the operational costs higher than anticipated.

Another frequent issue is control and autonomy. Franchisees might feel that the franchisor exerts excessive control over their operations, stifling their entrepreneurial spirit. Conversely, franchisors may feel that franchisees are not adequately adhering to brand standards or operational procedures, risking brand integrity.

Lastly, communication issues, whether due to lack of clarity, infrequency, or misunderstandings, can lead to conflicts. Misinterpretation of agreements or policies can also be a significant source of dispute.

Strategies for Conflict Resolution

Open Communication: The first step in resolving conflicts is to establish open lines of communication. Both parties should feel comfortable expressing concerns without fear of retribution.

Seek to Understand First: Each party should strive to understand the other's perspective. This empathetic approach can clarify misunderstandings and provide a foundation for collaborative problem-solving.

Use Mediation When Necessary: If internal efforts fail, third-party mediation can be a useful tool. A neutral mediator can help both parties see the broader picture and work towards a resolution that is acceptable to both.

Review and Amend Agreements if Needed: Sometimes, conflicts arise due to outdated or unclear agreements. Regularly reviewing and amending franchise agreements can prevent such issues.

Develop a Conflict Resolution Protocol: Having a predefined conflict resolution process can streamline the handling of disputes. This protocol should be fair, transparent, and known to all parties involved.

Importance of Ongoing Support and Training

Continuous support and training from the franchisor play a crucial role in minimizing conflicts. Regular training sessions keep franchisees up-to-date with the latest operational practices, marketing strategies, and compliance requirements. This ongoing education can help franchisees adapt to changing market conditions and meet the franchisor's expectations more effectively.

Support can also come in the form of regular performance reviews, where franchisors provide constructive feedback and guidance to help franchisees improve their operations. This approach not only helps in addressing potential issues before they escalate into conflicts but also reinforces the franchisee's commitment to the brand's success.

In conclusion, managing expectations and effectively resolving conflicts are critical for the longevity and success of the franchisor-franchisee relationship. By setting realistic expectations, understanding common conflict sources, employing effective resolution strategies, and ensuring ongoing support and training, both franchisors and franchisees can work towards a harmonious and mutually beneficial partnership.

This approach fosters a positive working environment where both parties feel valued, heard, and supported. It helps in building trust and loyalty, which are essential for navigating the complexities of the franchise business. When franchisors and franchisees are aligned in their goals, expectations, and methods of conflict resolution, the franchise system as a whole stands to benefit.

Moreover, by investing in ongoing training and support, franchisors not only equip their franchisees with the necessary tools and knowledge for success but also demonstrate a commitment to their franchisees' growth and wellbeing. This commitment is often reciprocated by franchisees through increased dedication to the brand and improved performance.

Effective conflict resolution and expectation management also contribute to the overall health of the franchise network. A network characterized by cooperative and supportive relationships is more resilient, adaptable, and capable of collective growth. It can better withstand market fluctuations and external challenges, ensuring long-term sustainability and success.

In essence, the ability to manage expectations and resolve conflicts effectively is not just a skill but a strategic asset in the franchising world. It enhances the franchisor-franchisee relationship, ensuring that both parties can work together effectively to achieve their shared vision of success. This collaborative and proactive approach is key to building a robust, dynamic, and thriving franchise system.

Case Studies of Successful Franchisor-Franchisee Relationships

The franchising world is filled with stories of remarkable partnerships that have led to tremendous business success. In this section, we delve into several case studies of successful franchisor-franchisee relationships, examining the models they used, key factors contributing to their success, and lessons that can be learned from these real-world examples. The section will also include insights from interviews and testimonials from both franchisors and franchisees.

Case Study 1: McDonald's – A Model of Systematic

Success

Franchise Model Analysis: McDonald's is a prime example of a successful franchise model. It's a system based on standardized procedures, ensuring consistency in product and service across all locations. The company provides extensive training and support to franchisees, emphasizing quality control, cleanliness, and service efficiency.

Key Success Factors: The success of McDonald's franchisees hinges on adherence to the franchise's strict operational guidelines, combined with local marketing efforts. The franchisor's support system, which includes training, marketing, and operational assistance, has been pivotal.

Lessons and Best Practices: A key takeaway from McDonald's is the importance of maintaining brand consistency while allowing for localized marketing strategies. Their business model underscores the significance of comprehensive training and support in fostering successful franchisor-franchisee relationships.

Franchisee Testimonial: A McDonald's franchisee highlighted the importance of the franchisor's ongoing support and training, which helped them adapt to local market needs while maintaining brand standards.

Case Study 2: Anytime Fitness – Flexibility and Support

Franchise Model Analysis: Anytime Fitness has made a name for itself in the fitness industry by offering a flexible and supportive franchise model. The brand stands out for its 24/7 gym access and a strong focus on community and member experience.

Key Success Factors: The success of Anytime Fitness franchises lies in the franchisor's ability to provide flexibility in operations while ensuring strong brand identity. The franchisor provides extensive support in real estate, finance, training, and marketing.

* * *

Lessons and Best Practices: Anytime Fitness demonstrates the importance of aligning franchisor support with the unique needs of franchisees, particularly in local market engagement and customization within the brand's framework.

Franchisee Testimonial: Franchisees of Anytime Fitness often cite the balance of autonomy in local decision-making and the robust support from the franchisor as key to their success.

Case Study 3: RE/MAX – Empowering Entrepreneurship

Franchise Model Analysis: RE/MAX, a global real estate network, has fostered a successful franchise model by empowering its franchisees. The model provides substantial autonomy to franchisees to run their operations, coupled with a strong brand and global network.

Key Success Factors: The success of RE/MAX franchisees can be attributed to the entrepreneurial freedom they enjoy, combined with the support and recognition of a powerful global brand. The franchisor offers extensive training, marketing tools, and a technology platform, while encouraging franchisees to innovate and adapt to their local markets.

Lessons and Best Practices: RE/MAX's approach highlights the importance of balancing franchisor support with franchisee autonomy. It shows that empowering franchisees to make local decisions can lead to greater motivation and success, especially in industries where local market knowledge is crucial.

Franchisee Testimonial: A RE/MAX franchise owner shared how the freedom to tailor their business to the local market, along with access to world-class resources and brand recognition, has been instrumental in their success.

Case Study 4: Subway – Customization and Collaboration

* * *

Franchise Model Analysis: Subway, one of the largest fast-food chains in the world, operates on a franchise model that emphasizes customization and collaboration. Franchisees are encouraged to tailor their menu and operations to local tastes and preferences.

Key Success Factors: Subway's success can be attributed to its collaborative approach and its focus on customization. The franchisor provides a proven business model, training, marketing support, and operational guidelines, while encouraging franchisees to provide feedback and suggestions.

Lessons and Best Practices: Subway's model demonstrates the effectiveness of a collaborative approach where franchisees' input is valued and used for mutual benefit. It shows that customization to local markets can be a key differentiator in a competitive industry.

Franchisee Testimonial: A franchisee shared how the ability to adapt their menu and store to local preferences, along with the franchisor's comprehensive support, has been key to attracting and retaining customers.

Case Study 5: Marriott International – Brand Strength and Operational Excellence

Franchise Model Analysis: Marriott International, a leading name in the hotel industry, operates a franchise model that balances strict operational standards with local market adaptation. The brand is known for its operational excellence and customer service.

Key Success Factors: The strength of the Marriott brand, along with its focus on operational excellence and customer service, has been central to the success of its franchisees. The franchisor provides rigorous training, quality control standards, and global marketing, ensuring a consistent guest experience worldwide.

Lessons and Best Practices: Marriott's approach illustrates the importance of maintaining high standards in service and operations while allowing franchisees to incorporate local elements. This balance is key in the hospitality industry, where customer experience is paramount.

Franchisee Testimonial: A Marriott franchisee emphasized the value of the brand's global recognition and the operational support provided, which significantly contributed to their high occupancy rates and customer satisfaction.

These case studies of successful franchisor-franchisee relationships across various industries reveal several common themes. The importance of a strong, supportive franchisor, the need for adherence to operational standards, and the benefits of allowing for local market customization are recurrent factors contributing to the success of these partnerships.

From fast food to fitness, real estate to hospitality, these examples showcase that while the specifics of each industry and franchise model may differ, the fundamentals of a successful franchisor-franchisee relationship remain consistent. They revolve around mutual respect, open communication, support and training, and a shared commitment to brand values and customer satisfaction.

By learning from these successful models and understanding the key factors that contributed to their achievements, prospective franchisors and franchisees can gain valuable insights into building and sustaining their own fruitful partnerships. These case studies not only serve as inspiration but also as practical guides for navigating the complex yet rewarding world of franchising.

Conclusion

As we reach the conclusion of our exploration into the franchisor-franchisee relationship, it's clear that the strength of this partnership is not just a contributor to success; it is a fundamental requirement for the flourishing of both entities in the complex tapestry of the franchise business model. This relationship, rooted in mutual respect, clear communication, and shared goals, forms the backbone of a franchise's ability to thrive in competitive markets.

* * *

The essence of a successful franchisor-franchisee relationship lies in the understanding that both parties are integral to each other's success. For franchisors, the network of franchisees is the vehicle through which their brand and vision are brought to life and delivered to a diverse range of markets. For franchisees, the franchisor provides the framework, resources, and brand reputation essential for kick-starting and sustaining their entrepreneurial journey.

Throughout this exploration, it has been evident that several key factors contribute to this symbiotic relationship. Open and effective communication stands as a pillar, ensuring that expectations are managed, conflicts are resolved constructively, and that the flow of information is continuous and productive. The importance of setting realistic expectations cannot be overstated – it lays the groundwork for a relationship based on transparency and trust.

Collaboration and mutual support emerge as another cornerstone. Whether through regular training, sharing of best practices, or joint problem-solving, these collaborative efforts reinforce the partnership and drive collective success. The highlighted case studies of successful franchise models further illuminate the path to achieving this harmonious relationship. They show how fostering a culture of mutual respect, support, and shared objectives leads to a prosperous and resilient franchise system.

Both franchisors and franchisees must remain committed to the core values and objectives of the franchise, while being flexible enough to adapt to new challenges and opportunities. This might involve embracing new technologies, responding to changing consumer behaviors, or exploring innovative business strategies.

Additionally, the importance of ongoing support and training cannot be underestimated. It ensures that franchisees are well-equipped to meet the demands of their markets and that franchisors remain in tune with the needs and challenges faced by their franchisees.

In closing, the franchisor-franchisee relationship is a dynamic and multifaceted one, demanding attention, effort, and a deep understanding of mutual needs and goals. By fostering a relationship characterized by open communication, collaboration, and mutual support, franchisors and franchisees can create a strong foundation for enduring success. This partnership is not just a contractual agreement; it is a shared journey towards achieving a common vision – the growth and prosperity of the brand and the individual businesses that comprise it.

CHAPTER NINE
EVALUATING YOUR FRANCHISE'S SUCCESS

In the competitive and ever-evolving world of franchising, the evaluation of a franchise's success is a continuous journey that drives growth and adaptation. This chapter opens with an overview of why evaluating franchise success is critical and how continuous assessment can become the engine for sustainable growth and strategic adaptation in the franchising landscape.

The evaluation of a franchise's success goes beyond mere profit margins and revenue growth. It encompasses a broader spectrum that includes market position, customer satisfaction, brand consistency, and alignment with evolving market trends. In the franchising model, where the success of individual franchise units directly impacts the reputation and growth of the overall brand, such evaluations gain an even greater significance.

Regular assessment of a franchise's performance serves multiple crucial functions. Firstly, it provides a clear picture of where the franchise stands in terms of meeting its business objectives. This includes not only financial metrics but also qualitative measures such as customer loyalty and brand strength. Secondly, it helps identify areas of improvement or potential risks that might have been overlooked. For instance, a dip in customer satisfaction scores in certain locations could indicate operational issues or a misalignment with customer expectations.

Moreover, these evaluations are instrumental in benchmarking a franchise's performance against industry standards and competitors. In an industry where staying ahead means keeping pace with or outperforming peers, understanding one's position in the market is invaluable for strategic planning and decision-making.

How Continuous Assessment Drives Growth and Adaptation

Continuous assessment in franchising is akin to navigating a ship in dynamic waters. It involves constantly monitoring various aspects of the business, from sales and customer feedback to operational efficiency and market trends. This ongoing process allows franchisors and franchisees to make informed, timely decisions that drive growth and ensure the franchise remains relevant and competitive.

Growth in franchising is not just about expanding the number of units; it's about sustainable, qualitative growth that enhances the brand's value and market presence. Continuous assessment helps identify successful strategies and practices that can be replicated across the franchise network, ensuring uniformity in quality and service. It also aids in recognizing the unique strengths and challenges of different franchise units, allowing for tailored support and resources where needed.

Adaptation is another critical component fueled by continuous assessment. In a landscape shaped by changing consumer behaviors, technological advancements, and economic shifts, the ability to adapt swiftly and effectively is key to a franchise's longevity. Regular evaluations provide the insights needed to pivot strategies, whether it's in marketing, product offerings, or operational methods, to stay aligned with market demands and opportunities.

Furthermore, continuous assessment nurtures a culture of innovation within the franchise system. By regularly reviewing performance and market trends, franchisors and franchisees are encouraged to think creatively, experiment with new ideas, and embrace innovative approaches that can lead to breakthroughs and set the franchise apart in a crowded market.

* * *

In conclusion, the evaluation of franchise success is a multifaceted and ongoing process that plays a critical role in the growth and adaptation of the franchise model. By embracing continuous assessment, franchisors and franchisees can ensure they are not just reacting to changes in the market but proactively steering their franchise towards long-term success and sustainability. This approach is essential for any franchise aiming to thrive and expand its footprint in today's dynamic business world.

Monitoring Performance and Adapting Strategies

In the dynamic world of franchising, monitoring performance through Key Performance Indicators (KPIs) and adapting business strategies accordingly is crucial for sustained success. This section delves into the significance of KPIs, how franchises can respond to performance data, and presents case studies of franchises that have successfully adapted their strategies.

Key Performance Indicators (KPIs) for Franchises

Identifying and Tracking Essential Metrics: KPIs are vital in measuring a franchise's performance and health. These metrics offer tangible data points to assess how well a franchise unit is meeting its predetermined goals. Essential KPIs for franchises typically include:

Sales and Revenue Growth: This is the primary indicator of a franchise's financial health. Tracking sales growth helps in evaluating the effectiveness of marketing strategies and understanding customer demand.

Customer Satisfaction and Retention Rates: Customer satisfaction metrics provide insights into the quality of service and products offered. High retention rates often indicate loyal customer bases, crucial for long-term success.

Operational Efficiency: This includes metrics like inventory turnover rates, labor costs as a percentage of sales, and average transaction values. Efficient operations are indicative of a well-run franchise.

Local Market Penetration: Understanding a franchise's share in the local market helps in assessing its competitiveness and effectiveness in reaching its target audience.

Brand Compliance: For franchises, maintaining brand consistency is crucial. Compliance metrics help ensure that each franchise unit adheres to the franchisor's standards.

Adapting Business Strategies

How to Respond to Performance Data: The interpretation and action taken in response to KPI data are as crucial as the data itself. Franchisors and franchisees need to:

Conduct Regular Reviews: Regularly scheduled reviews of KPIs allow franchisors and franchisees to stay informed and make timely decisions.

Identify Areas for Improvement: By analyzing KPIs, franchises can pinpoint areas that need attention, whether it's customer service, marketing efforts, or operational efficiency.

Set Realistic Goals: Based on KPIs, franchises can set achievable goals for improvement and growth.

Implement Targeted Strategies: Whether it's additional training, revised marketing tactics, or operational changes, strategies should be tailored to address the specific challenges or opportunities identified by KPIs.

Measure the Impact of Changes: After implementing new strategies, it's important to track their impact on relevant KPIs to ensure they are effective.

* * *

Case Studies: Successful Strategy Adaptations

1. Starbucks' Digital Transformation: Starbucks, one of the world's most recognizable coffeehouse chains, successfully adapted its strategy by embracing digital technology. Recognizing the trend towards mobile commerce, Starbucks introduced a mobile ordering and payment system. This adaptation not only improved customer experience but also increased sales efficiency. Starbucks' ability to leverage data from its digital platform to personalize offers further cemented its position as a leader in customer engagement within the food and beverage industry.

2. Domino's Pizza's Reinvention: Domino's Pizza exemplifies how a franchise can turn around its business by adapting strategies based on customer feedback. Facing criticism for the quality of their pizza, Domino's launched a transparent campaign admitting their shortcomings and reinvented their pizza recipe. This honest approach, coupled with investments in digital ordering systems, led to a remarkable turnaround in sales and customer perception.

3. Anytime Fitness's Focus on Convenience and Technology: Anytime Fitness, a global fitness franchise, adapted its business strategy to focus on convenience and the integration of technology. Recognizing the growing trend of wearable fitness technology and online fitness tracking, they implemented a strategy that integrated these technologies into their service offering. This adaptation not only attracted a tech-savvy clientele but also improved membership retention rates.

4. RE/MAX's Emphasis on Agent Training and Technology: In the real estate sector, RE/MAX demonstrated the importance of continually adapting strategies to stay ahead in a competitive market. They invested heavily in agent training and embraced new technologies for property listings and virtual tours, enhancing their service in an increasingly digital world. This focus on professional development and technology adoption has been key to their sustained success.

5. Subway's Menu Customization: Subway, the fast-food sandwich franchise, adapted its strategy by offering extensive menu customization, responding to the growing consumer demand for personalized dining experiences. This strategic shift helped Subway cater to a broader customer base with varied dietary preferences and needs, leading to increased customer satisfaction and sales.

In conclusion, the success of a franchise hinges not just on the robustness of its initial business model but on its ability to monitor performance through key metrics and adapt its strategies in response to this data. The case studies of Starbucks, Domino's, Anytime Fitness, RE/MAX, and Subway illustrate how franchises that are responsive to market trends, customer feedback, and technological advancements can achieve sustained growth and maintain a competitive edge in their respective industries. These examples serve as a testament to the power of agility and responsiveness in the ever-evolving world of franchising.

Customer Feedback and Market Analysis

In the dynamic environment of franchising, understanding and responding to customer needs and market trends are crucial for success. This section delves into effective methods for gathering and analyzing customer feedback, techniques for conducting thorough market analysis, and strategies for utilizing this invaluable data to drive improvements and adapt to changing market demands.

In today's customer-centric business landscape, gathering feedback is essential for franchises to stay relevant and competitive. Various methods can be employed:

Surveys and Questionnaires: These are powerful tools for collecting customer feedback. Digital platforms like SurveyMonkey or Google Forms allow franchises to design and distribute surveys easily. Key is to keep surveys short, relevant, and to the point to encourage higher response rates.

Comment Cards and Feedback Forms: Physical comment cards or online feedback forms can be used in franchise locations to gather immediate customer reactions.

* * *

Social Media and Online Reviews: Platforms like Facebook, Yelp, and Google My Business offer valuable insights into customer perceptions and experiences. Monitoring and responding to these reviews can provide direct feedback from a broad audience.

Focus Groups: Conducting focus groups gives an in-depth understanding of customer opinions and is particularly useful when considering new products or major changes.

Customer Interviews: One-on-one interviews, though resource-intensive, can provide deep insights into customer motivations and needs.

Analyzing the Feedback: Collecting feedback is just the first step. The crucial part is analyzing this data to identify trends, patterns, and areas for improvement. Tools like sentiment analysis software can help in interpreting large volumes of data from surveys and social media. The analysis should aim to uncover not just what customers like or dislike, but also why they feel a certain way about your product or service.

Market Analysis Techniques

Staying ahead in the dynamic franchise landscape demands a proactive approach to understanding market trends and customer demographics, which are crucial for maintaining a competitive edge.

Here are actionable strategies to achieve this:

Leverage Market Research Reports: Regularly delve into reports from industry experts like Nielsen or IBISWorld. These provide a comprehensive view of broader market trends, enabling informed strategic decisions.

Conduct Competitor Analysis: Consistently evaluate your competitors. This practice sheds light on market standards, emerging trends, and potential niches for differentiation, offering a blueprint for staying one step ahead.

Perform In-Depth Demographic Analysis: Utilize resources like the U.S. Census Bureau's database to gain insights into your target demographic's age, income, lifestyle, and purchasing habits. This knowledge is critical for customizing marketing approaches and product offerings.

Embrace Technological Analytics Tools: Implement tools like Google Analytics for a deep dive into website traffic and online customer behavior. Social media analytics can also unravel patterns in customer engagement and preferences.

Execute Local Market Surveys: Tailor surveys to your local market to grasp regional preferences and cultural nuances that might influence your business strategy.

Implementing Changes Based on Customer and Market Data:

Prioritize Data-Driven Decision Making: Base business modifications, whether in product/service adjustments, pricing strategies, or marketing shifts, on solid data extracted from customer feedback and market analysis.

Personalize the Customer Experience: Harness customer data to individualize interactions. Customized marketing messages and product suggestions can significantly boost customer satisfaction and loyalty.

Stay Agile to Market Trends: Be prepared to swiftly adjust your business strategies in response to evolving market trends, including adopting new technologies, expanding product lines, or optimizing operational processes.

Foster Continuous Innovation: Channel customer feedback into innovative endeavors. This could mean introducing novel products or services, experimenting with fresh marketing channels, or enhancing operational efficiency.

Invest in Training and Development: Utilize feedback to identify areas where staff training can elevate customer service and operational effectiveness.

By actively engaging with these strategies, franchises can not only adapt to the changing business environment but also position themselves as market leaders, attuned to the evolving needs of their customers and the market.

Case Studies of Effective Use of Feedback and Market Analysis

Chick-fil-A's Customer-Centric Approach: Chick-fil-A's success is partly attributed to its strong focus on customer service and feedback. The company regularly gathers customer feedback through various channels and uses this data to improve its service, menu offerings, and customer experience.

Starbucks' Market Adaptation: Starbucks has successfully adapted to varying market demands globally by understanding local cultures and preferences. Their localized menu offerings in different countries are an excellent example of using market analysis to cater to regional tastes.

Netflix's Use of Data Analytics: While not a traditional franchise, Netflix's use of data analytics for content and market analysis offers valuable lessons. By analyzing viewing patterns, feedback, and market trends, Netflix not only personalizes viewer recommendations but also makes informed decisions about which original content to produce.

Domino's Pizza's Menu Innovation: Domino's has effectively used customer feedback to transform its menu and service. After receiving negative feedback on the taste of their pizza, Domino's undertook a public campaign acknowledging the criticism and revamped its recipes, which led to a significant increase in customer satisfaction and sales.

Home Depot's Localized Product Strategy: Home Depot adjusts its product offerings based on local market analysis and customer preferences. In different geographical locations, they stock products that are relevant to the local climate and customer needs, demonstrating a keen understanding of demographic importance.

In conclusion, the effective gathering and analysis of customer feedback, coupled with a thorough understanding of market trends and demographics, are essential for the ongoing success and growth of a franchise. These practices not only help in making informed business decisions but also ensure that the franchise remains responsive and relevant to its customers. By implementing these strategies, franchises can adapt, innovate, and grow in alignment with customer needs and market dynamics, laying a strong foundation for long-term success.

Financial Metrics and Benchmarking

In the franchising sector, mastering financial metrics is not just about tracking profitability; it's a vital compass for strategic planning and ensuring the franchise's longevity. Here, we'll delve into the crucial financial metrics for franchises, highlight the importance of industry benchmarking, and outline a structured approach to regular financial assessments for lasting success.

Active Management of Key Financial Metrics:

1. **Intensive Revenue Monitoring:** Regularly track revenue both at individual franchise levels and across the entire network to gain a comprehensive view of financial performance. This step is fundamental to evaluating the business's financial pulse.

2. **Detailed Profit Margin Analysis:** Deeply analyze both gross and net profit margins. Gross profit margins reveal the cost-effectiveness of production or service provision, while net profit margins offer insights into the franchise's overall financial efficiency after all expenses.

3. **Rigorous Cost Management:** Vigilantly monitor and manage both fixed costs (like rent) and variable costs (such as labor and

inventory). Effective cost control is often the linchpin between a flourishing franchise and one that merely survives.

Benchmarking to Drive Competitive Advantage:

1. Engage in Industry Benchmarking: Regularly compare your franchise's financial metrics with industry standards and competitors. This practice is essential for identifying performance gaps and areas needing enhancement.

2. **Harness Industry Reports for Deeper Insights:** Leverage comprehensive industry reports from sources like IBISWorld or the National Franchise Association to obtain data crucial for effective benchmarking.

3. **Execute Competitive Performance Analyses:** Consistently evaluate your direct competitors to glean insights into market trends and operational efficiencies, offering opportunities for strategic improvements.

Structured Financial Health Assessments:

1. **Implement Systematic Financial Reviews:** Regularly (monthly, quarterly, and annually) review critical financial statements such as profit and loss accounts, balance sheets, and cash flow statements to ensure ongoing financial stability.

2. **Adopt Rigorous Auditing Practices:** Conduct both internal and external audits routinely to uncover any financial discrepancies, inefficiencies, or compliance issues, reinforcing financial integrity and adherence to franchisor standards.

3. **Monitor Financial KPIs Religiously:** Keep a close watch on financial Key Performance Indicators (KPIs) like same-store sales growth, average transaction values, and customer acquisition costs. These indicators can act as early warning systems for business performance and market positioning.

4. **Conduct Break-even Analysis:** Regularly determine your franchise's break-even point to set achievable sales targets and gauge financial feasibility.

5. **Strategize Debt Management:** Manage debts effectively by understanding the cost of capital and maintaining a balanced debt-to-equity ratio, crucial for financial health.

6. **Master Cash Flow Management:** Ensure robust cash flow management by timely receivables collection and strategic payables handling, crucial for operational liquidity.

By embracing these actionable strategies, franchises can not only maintain a sound financial foundation but also strategically steer towards sustainable growth and market competitiveness. These practices empower franchisees to make data-driven decisions, adapt to market changes, and secure a robust financial future.

Case Studies: Effective Financial Management in Franchising

McDonald's and Franchisee Profitability: McDonald's is known for its robust franchise model. A significant part of its success is attributed to its focus on franchisee profitability. McDonald's offers extensive support in financial planning and analysis, helping franchisees optimize their operations and improve profit margins.

7-Eleven's Turnaround Strategy: 7-Eleven's strategic focus on franchisee profitability led to a turnaround of its business. By implementing a centralized distribution system and optimizing their product mix based on local demographics, they improved margins for both franchisor and franchisees.

Subway's Cost Management: Subway's franchise model emphasizes cost control and efficiency. The company provides detailed guidelines on inventory management and operational practices to keep costs low, thereby improving the profitability of its franchisees.

* * *

The Role of Technology in Financial Management

In the fast-paced and competitive world of franchising, harnessing the power of financial management software is a game-changer. These sophisticated tools, such as QuickBooks, Xero, or specialized franchise management software, are essential in simplifying and streamlining financial tracking and analysis. They offer real-time insights into a franchise's financial performance, enabling franchisees and franchisors to make quick, data-driven decisions. The convenience of having a consolidated view of financial health at your fingertips cannot be overstated.

The role of data analytics in financial management is becoming increasingly pivotal. By employing advanced analytics, franchises can gain predictive insights that forecast sales trends, decode customer behavior, and understand market dynamics. This forward-looking approach is invaluable in shaping strategic decisions that align with future market movements and consumer demands.

In summary, mastering financial metrics is not just a necessity; it's a strategic imperative for any franchise's success. It's about conducting regular financial health checks, benchmarking against industry standards, and adopting robust financial management practices. These steps are vital to maintaining profitability and ensuring the sustainability of the franchise.

Staying informed and vigilant about financial indicators allows franchisors and franchisees to adeptly navigate the complexities of the business landscape. It's about being responsive to what the numbers are telling you and using this knowledge to guide your franchise towards sustained growth and long-term success. By integrating these advanced financial tools and analytical techniques into their operations, franchises can position themselves for a prosperous future.

This comprehensive approach to financial metrics and benchmarking allows franchises to not only keep pace with their competitors but also identify unique opportunities for innovation and expansion. Financial acumen, combined with strategic foresight, is what sets apart successful franchises in the competitive business landscape. By cultivating these financial management practices, franchises can build a strong foundation for resilience, adaptability, and enduring success.

Preparing for Future Trends and Market Shifts

To identify emerging market trends, franchises should leverage market research tools and data analytics. Platforms like Statista, Nielsen, and IBISWorld offer extensive industry reports and analyses, shedding light on new consumer behaviors, market demands, and potential areas for growth. Social media platforms and online forums are not just marketing tools but are also rich sources for understanding current consumer interests and behaviors. These digital platforms can offer real-time insights into shifting consumer preferences.

Conducting competitive analysis is another crucial strategy. Tools like SEMrush and Ahrefs can help analyze competitors' online strategies, revealing emerging trends and market shifts. Additionally, attending industry conferences and networking events can provide broader market perspectives. Importantly, franchises shouldn't overlook the value of direct customer feedback. Surveys, feedback forms, and digital interactions can be instrumental in understanding changing consumer needs.

When it comes to adapting to technological advances, franchises need to embrace digital transformation. Implementing cloud-based systems, AI-driven analytics, and CRM software can dramatically enhance operational efficiency and customer relationship management. Investing in e-commerce and mobile solutions is essential, considering the growing trend of online shopping. These platforms can open new revenue streams and improve customer accessibility. Additionally, leveraging social media and digital marketing tools is vital for brand promotion and customer engagement in today's digital age. Incorporating Internet of Things (IoT) and automation technologies can also streamline operations, reduce costs, and enhance customer experiences, especially in sectors like retail and hospitality.

For strategic planning and long-term growth, developing a flexible business model that can swiftly adapt to market changes is critical. This approach involves being open to new ideas, experimenting with different methods, and being prepared to pivot strategies when necessary. Fostering a culture of innovation within the franchise, where new ideas and creative solutions are actively pursued, can position the franchise to capitalize on future opportunities. Regular training and development programs ensure that employees are adept in the latest technologies and business practices, keeping the franchise at the cutting edge of industry developments. Engaging in scenario planning prepares franchises for various market conditions in the future. It involves envisioning different market scenarios and developing strategic responses for each.

In conclusion, understanding and responding to market trends, embracing technological advancements, and proactive strategic planning are crucial for any franchise's future success. By staying informed, agile, and innovative, franchises can navigate the complexities of the market and steer their businesses towards sustained growth and relevance in an ever-evolving business landscape.

Preparing for the Unknown: Flexibility in Strategy

In recent years, unforeseen challenges such as the global pandemic have underlined the critical importance of maintaining a flexible strategy in the franchise industry. To stay ahead in this dynamic environment, franchises must focus on several key areas.

Firstly, building resilience is essential. This means developing a business model that can withstand market shocks. Diversification of revenue streams is a vital aspect of this resilience, as it allows franchises to remain robust even when one area of the business faces challenges. Additionally, robust contingency planning is indispensable. This involves preparing for various scenarios and having clear, actionable plans in place to address potential market disruptions.

Another critical element is embracing change. Franchises should cultivate an organizational mindset that views challenges as opportunities for growth and innovation. This mindset encourages adaptability and a proactive approach to evolving market conditions. It involves being open to new ideas, strategies, and practices that can help the franchise navigate through turbulent times.

Continuous learning and development play a pivotal role in staying current with global trends and innovations. Franchises need to invest in regular training and skill development for both leadership and staff. This ongoing educational process ensures that everyone within the franchise is equipped to adapt to new technologies, methodologies, and market shifts.

Investing in sustainable practices is also becoming increasingly important. With the growing global focus on environmental sustainability, adopting eco-friendly practices and aligning with green initiatives is not just a moral responsibility but also a smart business strategy. It can lead to improved operational efficiency and meet the rising consumer demand for sustainable options. This commitment to sustainability can also enhance the brand's image and appeal to a broader customer base.

In conclusion, preparing for future trends and market shifts is about proactively predicting and adapting to these changes. Staying informed, embracing new technologies, fostering a culture of innovation, and maintaining strategic flexibility are key to thriving in the face of future challenges and opportunities. Franchises that can successfully navigate these elements will not only survive but also flourish, securing a competitive edge in an ever-evolving business landscape.

Case Studies of Successful Adaptation and Growth

The franchising world is replete with stories of adaptation and triumph, offering valuable lessons for aspiring and established franchisees and franchisors alike. This section presents case studies of franchises that have successfully navigated market shifts and technological changes, outlining the key takeaways from their experiences.

Case Study 1: Starbucks – Embracing Digital Innovation

Real-World Example: Starbucks, a global leader in the coffee industry, has consistently stayed ahead of market trends, particularly in digital innovation. The launch of their Mobile Order & Pay app revolutionized customer service by reducing waiting times and enhancing customer experience.

Lessons Learned:

- **Customer Convenience is Key:** Starbucks' app made ordering convenient, showing the importance of adapting to consumer lifestyle changes.
- **Data-Driven Decision Making:** The app also provides Starbucks with valuable customer data, which they use to personalize offers and understand consumer preferences.

Case Study 2: Domino's Pizza – Reinvention and Technology Integration

Real-World Example: Domino's Pizza is an exemplary story of a franchise that turned its fortunes around through strategic adaptation. Faced with criticism over food quality, Domino's revamped its recipes and transparently communicated this change to customers. They also embraced technology, allowing customers to order via Twitter, text, smart TV, and even by emoji.

Lessons Learned:

- **Transparency Builds Trust:** Domino's honest communication about their recipe changes garnered public respect.
- **Technological Adaptation is Crucial:** The integration of

diverse technological platforms for ordering positioned Domino's as an innovative leader in the food industry.

Case Study 3: Anytime Fitness – Adapting to Health and Fitness Trends

Real-World Example: Anytime Fitness has adeptly navigated the health and fitness industry by adapting to current trends. They have shifted towards holistic health solutions, offering personalized training and wellness programs.

Lessons Learned:

- **Adapt to Industry Trends:** Anytime Fitness's shift to holistic health services shows the importance of evolving with industry trends.
- **Personalization Appeals to Consumers:** Offering personalized fitness solutions helped them to cater to individual customer needs, enhancing client retention.

Case Study 4: RE/MAX – Leveraging Technology in Real Estate

Real-World Example: RE/MAX, a global real estate giant, has effectively used technology to stay ahead in a highly competitive market. They have implemented virtual house tours and AI-driven property suggestions, enhancing the buying experience in the digital age.

Lessons Learned:

- **Innovative Use of Technology Enhances Service:** The adoption of virtual tours and AI in real estate processes has set RE/MAX apart from its competitors.
- **Stay Ahead of Technological Curves:** Continuous investment in new technologies is essential to remain relevant and competitive.

* * *

Case Study 5: McDonald's – Strategic Market Adaptation

Real-World Example: McDonald's has shown remarkable adaptability in diverse global markets. They customize their menu to cater to regional tastes while maintaining their core product offerings, balancing global brand consistency with local relevance.

Lessons Learned:

- **Local Adaptation is Crucial for Global Brands:** McDonald's success in different markets is partly due to its sensitivity to local cultural and culinary preferences.

- **Maintain Core Brand Values:** While adapting to local markets, maintaining core brand values and offerings is vital for brand recognition and loyalty.

These case studies illustrate that successful franchises are those that are not only responsive to market changes and consumer trends but are also proactive in anticipating and adapting to these shifts. Whether it's through technological innovation, market adaptation, service diversification, or transparent communication, these franchises have demonstrated resilience and agility in a constantly evolving business landscape.

The key takeaways from these success stories underscore the importance of customer-centric strategies, embracing technology, and the willingness to reinvent and innovate. These elements are crucial for any franchise looking to achieve long-term growth and success in today's dynamic market environment.

* * *

Conclusion

As we conclude our exploration into the world of franchising, it's evident that the ability to evaluate, adapt, and remain agile is crucial for enduring success. This journey through various aspects of franchising - from monitoring performance to embracing technological changes - underscores a central theme: the franchising landscape is dynamic, and success in this field demands responsiveness and flexibility.

The process of continual evaluation, through methods like analyzing key performance indicators, gathering customer feedback, and conducting market analysis, is vital. It provides franchises with the insights needed to make informed decisions and strategize effectively. This ongoing assessment allows franchises to identify areas of strength to build upon, as well as areas requiring improvement or innovation.

Adaptation, a natural progression from evaluation, is what keeps franchises relevant and competitive. The case studies of franchises like Starbucks, Domino's, and McDonald's highlight how adapting to consumer preferences, technological advancements, and market trends is not just beneficial but essential. Whether it's revamping product offerings, integrating digital solutions, or customizing services to local markets, the ability to adapt defines the growth trajectory of a franchise.

The ever-changing market environment, characterized by evolving consumer behaviors, technological advancements, and unpredictable economic shifts, requires franchises to be agile. Agility in this context means more than quick reactions to market changes; it involves a proactive approach to foreseeing and preparing for future trends. It's about cultivating a culture of innovation where new ideas are welcomed and tested, and where flexibility is ingrained in the business model.

Staying agile also means prioritizing continuous learning and development, both at the franchisor and franchisee levels. Investing in training, embracing new technologies, and staying attuned to global trends are practices that equip franchises to navigate the complexities of the market.

In summary, the key to franchising success lies in a balanced approach of steadfast adherence to core brand values and an adaptable strategy to meet market demands. This equilibrium ensures that franchises can maintain their brand identity while staying relevant and competitive. The future of franchising belongs to those who can effectively evaluate their performance, adapt to changes with agility, and continually evolve with the market. In this dynamic business landscape, the ability to pivot and grow will continue to be the hallmark of successful franchising.

CHAPTER TEN
CONCLUSION AND MOVING FORWARD

As we draw the curtains on this comprehensive exploration of the franchising journey, it's essential to look back briefly on the path we've traversed and, more importantly, to focus on the road ahead. The world of franchising, as we've seen, is dynamic and multifaceted, presenting unique challenges and abundant opportunities. This final chapter aims not only to recap the key aspects of franchising but also to emphasize the importance of forward-thinking and preparedness to navigate the future.

The journey through the world of franchising, as delineated in this book, has taken us through various critical aspects. We started by understanding the basic principles of franchising, the roles of franchisors and franchisees, and the importance of selecting the right franchise. We delved into the nuances of the franchisor-franchisee relationship, underscoring the significance of communication, cooperation, and mutual growth.

We also explored the pivotal role of customer feedback and market analysis in shaping a franchise's strategies and adapting to changing market trends. Financial management, an indispensable component of franchising success, was also examined in detail, highlighting the need for effective financial planning, benchmarking, and regular health checks.

The book also tackled the challenges and opportunities presented by emerging market trends and technological advancements. We learned how successful franchises have adapted to these changes, demonstrating agility and innovative thinking. This journey through the franchising landscape has provided a wealth of knowledge, insights, and practical strategies, equipping readers with the tools needed to thrive in the franchising world.

The Importance of Looking Ahead and Preparing for Future Challenges and Opportunities

The ability to look ahead and prepare for future challenges and opportunities is what separates successful franchises from the rest. The franchising landscape is constantly evolving with shifts in consumer behavior, technological advancements, and economic changes. This environment demands not just a reactive approach but a proactive strategy that anticipates and adapts to these changes.

To stay competitive, franchises must embrace change and be open to innovation. This means being willing to test new ideas, explore emerging markets, and adopt new technologies that can enhance operational efficiency and customer experience. Franchises that are quick to adapt to change are often the ones that not only survive but thrive, even in turbulent times.

The franchising journey is one of continual learning and growth. It's crucial for both franchisors and franchisees to stay informed about industry trends, consumer demands, and best practices. This constant learning process enables them to make informed decisions, refine their business strategies, and seize new opportunities as they arise.

Resilience is key in franchising. This involves developing a business model that can withstand market fluctuations, economic downturns, and unexpected challenges. It means having contingency plans in place, diversifying revenue streams, and maintaining a strong financial foundation.

The success of a franchise also hinges on the strength of its relationships - with customers, employees, suppliers, and other stakeholders. Nurturing these relationships, understanding their needs, and responding to them effectively can help in building a loyal customer base and a supportive network that can be crucial during challenging times.

Looking ahead also involves considering the long-term impact of business practices. Adopting sustainable and ethical practices not only appeals to the growing demographic of environmentally and socially conscious consumers but also ensures the long-term viability and social responsibility of the franchise.

As we conclude this journey, it's important to recognize that franchising, at its core, is about partnership, innovation, and growth. Whether you are a prospective franchisee contemplating this venture or a seasoned franchisor looking to expand, the principles and insights explored in this book are intended to guide and inspire your path forward.

The world of franchising offers a unique blend of entrepreneurial spirit and collaborative business model. It presents a pathway to ownership and success, but one that requires commitment, adaptability, and a forward-thinking mindset. With the right approach, strategies, and mindset, the opportunities in franchising are limitless.

In moving forward, embrace the challenges as opportunities for growth, stay adaptable to the ever-changing business landscape, and remain committed to continuous improvement and ethical practices. The journey of franchising is one of discovery and development, and the future holds incredible potential for those prepared to navigate its course.

Key Takeaways from the Franchising Journey

In the world of franchising, understanding the key elements that drive success is crucial. This section provides a summary of the crucial lessons learned about franchising, reflects on the core principles of adaptability, customer focus, and continuous improvement, and reiterates the importance of financial management, market analysis, and relationship building.

* * *

To thrive in the franchising world, it's essential to grasp the franchise model's nuances, choose the right franchise, foster a strong franchisor-franchisee relationship, adhere to system standards, and understand the local market. Here are specific, actionable insights and tips drawn from the book to guide you:

1.   **Understanding the Franchise Model**

   - **Action Steps:** Attend franchising workshops and seminars to deepen your understanding of the franchisor-franchisee dynamic. Regularly communicate with your franchisor to stay aligned with their vision and expectations.
   - **Tip:** Use resources provided by the franchisor, like operation manuals and training programs, to fully grasp the business model.

2.   **Choosing the Right Franchise**

   - **Action Steps:** Conduct a self-assessment to determine your interests, skills, and financial capability. Research various franchises, focusing on those that align with your assessment.
   - **Tip:** Utilize franchising expos and online directories to explore options. Consult with current franchisees to get firsthand insights.

3.   **The Franchisor-Franchisee Relationship**

   - **Action Steps:** Establish regular communication channels with your franchisor. Attend franchisee meetings and engage in collaborative forums.
   - **Tip:** Practice transparent communication, especially regarding challenges and successes, to foster trust and mutual understanding.

4.   **Adherence to System Standards**

   - **Action Steps:** Regularly review the franchisor's guidelines to ensure compliance. Conduct internal audits to monitor adherence to these standards.
   - **Tip:** Implement staff training sessions focusing on the

importance of maintaining brand consistency and quality standards.

5. **Local Market Understanding**

- **Action Steps:** Conduct local market research to understand customer demographics and preferences. Adapt marketing strategies to resonate with the local community.
- **Tip:** Engage in community events and local initiatives to gain a deeper understanding of the market and build brand presence.

6. **Adaptability to Market Changes**

- **Action Steps:** Stay informed about industry trends and consumer behavior. Be ready to pivot strategies in response to market feedback and changes.
- **Tip:** Use customer feedback mechanisms and market research tools to gauge and respond to changing market demands.

7. **Customer-Centric Approach**

- **Action Steps:** Implement regular customer satisfaction surveys. Train your staff in customer service excellence.
- **Tip:** Personalize customer interactions and tailor your services or products to meet specific customer needs.

8. **Continuous Improvement**

- **Action Steps:** Regularly review and update your products and services. Encourage and implement feedback from customers and staff.
- Tip: Stay open to innovation and be willing to test new ideas for improving your business operations and offerings.

9. Financial Management

- **Action Steps:** Develop a comprehensive financial plan. Regularly review financial statements and conduct audits.
- Tip: Utilize financial management software for accurate tracking and analysis. Seek advice from financial experts when

necessary.

10. Market Analysis

- **Action Steps:** Continually gather data on competitors and industry trends. Use this data to inform strategic decisions.
- **Tip:** Leverage tools like Google Analytics for online market analysis and customer behavior tracking.

11. Relationship Building

- Action Steps: Foster strong relationships with all stakeholders – customers, employees, suppliers, and the community.
- Tip: Regularly engage in team-building activities and community service projects to strengthen these relationships.

By implementing these strategies and tips, you'll be better equipped to navigate the complexities of franchising, ensuring sustained growth and success in your venture.

Case Examples Illustrating Key Takeaways

McDonald's Focus on System Standards: McDonald's success as a franchise lies in its strict adherence to system standards across the globe, ensuring a consistent customer experience.

Subway's Adaptation to Health Trends: Subway's shift to include healthier options on its menu in response to changing consumer health trends is an excellent example of adaptability in franchising.

7-Eleven's Innovative Customer-Focused Strategies: 7-Eleven's introduction of tech-savvy solutions like mobile apps for customer convenience showcases their commitment to continuous improvement and customer focus.

RE/MAX and Financial Management: RE/MAX's emphasis on robust financial training for its franchisees underlines the importance of financial acumen in the success of a franchise.

Anytime Fitness and Community Engagement: Anytime Fitness's strategy of building community-focused gyms, where emphasis is placed on creating a supportive environment, demonstrates the significance of relationship building in franchising.

The franchising journey is complex and multifaceted, yet rich with opportunities for growth and success. The key takeaways from this journey – understanding the franchise model, the importance of a strong franchisor-franchisee relationship, adaptability to market changes, customer-centric approaches, continuous improvement, astute financial management, in-depth market analysis, and robust relationship building – are essential ingredients for a prosperous franchising venture.

Embracing these principles will not only guide current and prospective franchisees and franchisors in navigating the challenges of franchising but will also equip them to seize opportunities and achieve sustained success.

Planning for Long-Term Success and Sustainability

Ensuring the longevity and health of a franchise requires a multifaceted approach, combining strategic planning, continual adaptation, and a focus on customer experience.

At the foundation of a thriving franchise lies robust business planning. A comprehensive business plan, encompassing detailed financial projections, market analysis, and a clear understanding of the target customer base, is crucial. However, it's equally important for this plan to be flexible, allowing the franchise to adapt to the ever-changing market conditions.

Effective risk management is another critical aspect. This involves conducting regular SWOT analyses to identify strengths, weaknesses, opportunities, and threats, thereby recognizing potential challenges. Developing strategies to mitigate these risks and having contingency plans for unforeseen events, such as economic downturns or market disruptions, ensures a franchise's resilience.

A key to maintaining high operational standards and staying competitive is ongoing training and support. Continual education of franchisees and their staff on new products, marketing strategies, and operational efficiencies keeps the business at the forefront of industry developments.

Innovation and adaptation are indispensable in the dynamic franchising world. Staying competitive might mean regularly updating product lines, embracing new technologies, or revising service offerings in response to evolving customer needs. This innovation extends to the customer experience as well. Providing high-quality products or services and ensuring a positive brand image are fundamental for building customer loyalty and attracting new business.

Underpinning all these efforts is the importance of strategic planning and ongoing market research. Setting long-term goals and regularly revisiting and adjusting the strategic plan in line with market changes lays a roadmap for future success. Continuously researching the market, keeping abreast of industry trends, competitor activities, and changing customer preferences are vital. Utilizing tools like market research surveys, social media monitoring, and customer feedback mechanisms provides invaluable insights.

Additionally, staying ahead of industry trends is crucial. Proactively identifying and adapting to these trends gives franchises a competitive edge. This proactive stance involves not just following current trends but also anticipating future shifts. Engaging in industry conferences, subscribing to trade publications, and actively participating in professional networks are effective methods to stay informed and ahead of the curve.

In essence, the health and longevity of a franchise depend on a balanced mix of solid planning, continuous improvement, risk management, and staying in tune with industry dynamics. By embracing these strategies, franchises can navigate the complexities of the market, ensuring sustained growth and success.

* * *

Discussion on Sustainability Practices and Their Growing Relevance in the Franchising World

In the world of franchising, planning for long-term success and sustainability is a multifaceted endeavor that extends beyond mere business strategies to encompass sustainability, social responsibility, and employee wellbeing.

The increasing trend towards sustainability in business is reshaping how franchises operate. Embracing eco-friendly practices offers dual benefits: it helps protect the environment and can also lead to significant cost savings and an enhanced brand image. This could involve using sustainable materials, minimizing waste, or implementing energy-efficient processes in day-to-day operations. By adopting these practices, franchises not only contribute positively to the environment but also appeal to a growing base of eco-conscious consumers.

Another critical aspect of a franchise's long-term strategy is its commitment to social responsibility. In today's consumer market, there's a noticeable shift towards brands that demonstrate a sense of social responsibility. Franchises have the opportunity to strengthen their community ties and enhance their social impact by engaging in local community projects, supporting charitable causes, or partnering with socially responsible suppliers. These initiatives not only build a positive brand image but also foster a sense of community and belonging, which can be invaluable for business growth.

Central to the health of a franchise is the wellbeing of its employees. A franchise that prioritizes the happiness and health of its employees is likely to see increased productivity and higher levels of customer service. Strategies to enhance employee wellbeing can range from offering fair wages and benefits to creating a positive and inclusive work environment. Ensuring a healthy work-life balance for employees is also crucial in maintaining a motivated and committed workforce.

In summary, the journey towards long-term success and sustainability in franchising involves a comprehensive approach that integrates robust business planning and effective risk management with continuous innovation and customer focus. However, it also requires an ongoing commitment to broader aspects such as market research, adapting to industry trends, and crucially, incorporating sustainability and social responsibility into the core business practices. By embracing these diverse yet interconnected strategies, franchises can secure their longevity, health, and relevance in an increasingly dynamic and evolving business landscape.

Exploring Further Franchise Opportunities

The franchising industry, diverse and ever-expanding, offers a plethora of opportunities for growth and diversification. For prospective franchisees and even seasoned ones looking to expand, identifying and evaluating new franchise opportunities is a critical process. This section aims to guide readers through the steps of discovering and assessing new franchising prospects, emphasizing the importance of market needs assessment, due diligence, and evaluating the viability of these ventures.

Research and Identification: The first step in exploring new franchise opportunities is comprehensive research. Prospective franchisees should start by identifying industries that are not only thriving but also align with their interests and expertise. Trade shows, franchising expos, and industry publications are excellent resources for understanding current trends and opportunities.

Utilize Franchising Portals and Consultants: Online franchising portals offer a wide array of information on various franchise opportunities. Additionally, consulting with franchising experts or brokers can provide valuable insights and recommendations based on individual preferences and market conditions.

Networking: Engaging with existing franchisees, attending franchising networking events, and joining relevant online forums and social media groups can provide first-hand insights into different franchise models and their performance.

* * *

Assessing Market Needs and Potential for Expansion or Diversification

Market Analysis: Understanding the market demand in your desired location is crucial. This involves analyzing the local customer base, demographics, competition, and economic conditions. Tools like market analysis software, local business reports, and demographic data can aid in this assessment.

Identifying Gaps in the Market: Look for market gaps that a new franchise could fill. Is there a demand for specific products or services that is not currently being met? Assessing unmet needs in the market can lead to profitable franchising opportunities.

Potential for Expansion or Diversification: For existing franchisees, it's important to consider how a new franchise would fit into their current portfolio. Would this new venture provide an opportunity for diversification, or would it complement and expand upon existing operations?

Tips on Due Diligence and Evaluating the Viability of New Franchise Ventures

1. Conduct Thorough Due Diligence: Investigating the franchise's history, financial performance, legal matters, and reputation is essential. This includes reviewing the Franchise Disclosure Document (FDD), understanding franchisor support systems, training, marketing, and operational assistance.

1. **Financial Assessment:** A detailed financial analysis of the franchise opportunity is crucial. This should include an examination of initial investment costs, ongoing fees, revenue projections, and break-even analysis. Tools like financial modeling software can assist in this assessment.

1. **Legal and Regulatory Considerations:** Understanding the legal and regulatory aspects of the franchise is paramount.

Consult with a franchise attorney to review contracts, franchisor obligations, territorial rights, and any state-specific franchising regulations.

1. **Talk to Existing Franchisees:** One of the best ways to gauge the viability of a franchise is to speak with current franchisees. Their experiences and insights can provide a realistic picture of what to expect and can highlight potential challenges and rewards.

1. **Evaluate Support and Training Programs:** The quality of training and support provided by the franchisor is a key determinant of success. Evaluate the comprehensiveness of these programs and their alignment with your needs and expectations.

1. **Consider Long-term Trends:** Assess whether the franchise aligns with long-term industry trends. It's crucial to invest in a franchise that is not only successful today but has the potential for sustained growth and relevance in the future.

While it's important to choose a franchise that aligns with personal interests and passions, balancing this with practical business considerations is vital. The most successful franchisees are those who can combine their enthusiasm for the business with a pragmatic approach to market demands and financial realities.

Understanding and assessing the risks associated with a new franchise venture is critical. This involves not just financial risk but also considering the time commitment, potential market shifts, and the personal impact of running the franchise.

Exploring new franchise opportunities is a journey that requires diligent research, thorough market analysis, and careful consideration of various factors. By conducting comprehensive due diligence, assessing market needs, and carefully evaluating the financial and operational aspects of potential franchises, prospective franchisees can make informed decisions that align with their goals, market conditions, and personal aspirations. The key to success in franchising lies in finding the right balance between passion, market demand, and financial viability, ensuring a rewarding and prosperous franchising journey.

Final Words

In the vibrant world of franchising, the journey is both exhilarating and demanding, offering a unique blend of entrepreneurship backed by the structure and support of an established brand. This path is not just about running a business; it's about creating something unique and personal, leveraging the strengths of the franchisor while imprinting your own entrepreneurial spirit. Whether starting anew or bringing years of experience, franchisees are encouraged to embrace the challenges and opportunities that come with this journey.

Success in franchising is marked by resilience—the ability to navigate through highs and lows. The journey is seldom straightforward, with its share of setbacks and triumphs. Resilience, the capacity to recover from difficulties, to learn from failures, and to persistently move forward, distinguishes those who realize their dreams from those who falter in the face of adversity.

Hard work and dedication are the cornerstones of success in the franchising world. While franchisors provide the framework and support, the success of the franchise predominantly hinges on the effort and commitment of the franchisee. Be prepared to invest time and effort to build and nurture a successful business.

Passion is the driving force in this journey. It's the energy that fuels daily operations and long-term goals, setting you apart and propelling your franchise towards success. A franchise thrived on an entrepreneur's passion for their business, their customers, and their products or services.

Continual learning and adaptation are crucial in an ever-evolving business landscape. Stay inquisitive and committed to learning. Keep abreast of industry trends, participate in franchising seminars and workshops, and continuously seek knowledge. Adaptability, the ability to adjust to changing market conditions, customer preferences, and technological advancements, is key in franchising. This flexibility enables you to effectively manage the ups and downs of the business environment, maintaining relevance and competitiveness.

One of the great benefits of being part of a franchise system is access to a wealth of resources from the franchisor. Fully utilize the training programs, marketing tools, and operational support offered. These resources are designed to aid your success, but it's up to you to make the most of them.

Building a strong support network is also vital. Connect with other franchisees, join franchising associations, and engage in community groups. Sharing experiences and advice with peers can offer valuable insights and support.

As you embark on or continue your franchising journey, remember to stay true to your core values. These should guide your business decisions and actions. Running a business in alignment with your personal and professional values leads to greater satisfaction and success. While dedication to your business is crucial, maintaining a work-life balance is equally important for sustaining the energy and focus needed to run a successful franchise.

Always keep the customer at the forefront of your strategy. Understanding and meeting their needs is essential for building brand loyalty and a strong reputation. And don't forget to celebrate your achievements along the way. Whether it's reaching a sales goal, opening a new location, or receiving positive customer feedback, acknowledging and celebrating these milestones keeps you motivated and inspired.

In conclusion, the franchising journey offers a balance between entrepreneurship and structured support, making it both rewarding and viable for many entrepreneurs. It's a journey marked by continuous evolution, ripe with opportunities for personal and professional growth. Embrace this path with passion, resilience, and an open mind, and the world of franchising offers immense possibilities for growth and fulfillment. With the lessons, strategies, and insights from this journey, you are well-equipped to navigate the challenges and seize the opportunities that come your way. The future of franchising is bright for those prepared to embrace it with enthusiasm and a relentless drive. Go forth, embrace the journey, and carve out your own success story.

About the Author

Fred Daphne, an accomplished writer and seasoned franchising expert, brings over two decades of rich experience to the fore. His impressive journey in the world of business began with a degree in Business Management, focused on Entrepreneurial Studies. This academic foundation deeply ingrained a comprehensive understanding of the business landscape in him.

Launching his career amidst the vibrant hustle of New York, Daphne ventured into the multifaceted world of franchising. Here, he engaged with diverse franchise models, from bustling fast-food chains to major retail brands. It was in this dynamic environment that he developed a keen interest in the transformative role of technology in traditional business practices, driving him to further his education with an MBA, emphasizing Information Systems.

Beyond the corporate realm, Daphne expanded his horizon internationally, consulting for global franchises aiming to modernize and innovate. His expertise has revitalized numerous enterprises, guiding them to integrate advanced technologies, thus streamlining their operations and appealing to contemporary markets.

Dedicated to empowering others through knowledge sharing, Daphne is a prolific writer for industry publications and a sought-after speaker at international franchising conferences. His articles are renowned for distilling complex technological trends into practical, actionable business strategies.

Away from the technological whirlwind and business strategizing,

Daphne finds solace in sailing, embracing the tranquility of the sea as a refreshing contrast to the fast-paced franchising world. He is also deeply committed to mentoring young entrepreneurs, driven by the belief that the next groundbreaking innovation in franchising is on the horizon, ready to be unveiled by a blend of passion and technological acumen.

www.ingramcontent.com/pod-product-compliance
Lightning Source LLC
Chambersburg PA
CBHW072158290526
45794CB00004B/1560